THE
VINEYARD
DNA

ESSENTIAL HISTORY, VALUES, & PRACTICES
OF THE VINEYARD MOVEMENT

vineyardresources®

Vineyard Resources
5115 Grove West Blvd.
Stafford, TX 77477
www.vineyardresources.com
sales@vineyardresources.com

Ordering Information:

Quantity sales. Special discounts are available on quantity purchases by churches, organizations, and others. For details, contact the publisher at the address above.

Orders by U.S. trade bookstores and wholesalers. Please contact Vineyard Resources: Tel: (800) 852-8463 or visit www.vineyardresources.com.

First Edition

DEDICATION

This book is dedicated to Vineyard pastors and leaders around the world.

We've seen firsthand the dedication you pour into your community to see the Gospel expressed in your context.

You are living the Kingdom dream each week with your congregation in your town, city, and nation – and we believe that Jesus is pleased with your desire to love this world in His name.

We're cheering you on.

Vineyard Resources

TABLE OF CONTENTS

INTRODUCTION

"I've experienced so much with God and others over all these years in the Vineyard – how will I ever communicate any of it to my staff or congregation, or to the next generation of leaders?"

This pastor, like so many others we've spoken with over the years, was expressing a longing for those with whom they do life as Christians to understand the profoundly life-changing experience being in the Vineyard has been.

With so many new staff and church members who had never heard of John Wimber, never read *Power Evangelism*, and never sang *Faithful One* at the top of their lungs as they climbed over chairs to pray for people at a *Signs & Wonders* conference, these leaders are wondering how they could ever communicate the power, the joy, the passion of leading with others in the unique family that is the Vineyard!

Whether you are that pastor, that staff leader, or that Vineyard church member, this book was compiled with you in mind. While only those who have experienced God's Kingdom coming during their time in the Vineyard can tell the rich stories of personal encounter so vital to the transfer of insight, history, and values, this book attempts to provide a launch point for the sharing of those stories.

In the following pages we have compiled material from some of our best writing over the past few years; writings that summarize our history, theology, distinctives, values, and practices as a movement. In other words, this book is primarily a collection of writings we've released in the past few years, each focused on the unique topic that guides each chapter.

THE VINEYARD DNA

While we've tied these chapters together into one handbook, there may be moments you notice a change in tone or a unique approach to the content. That is because the compiled material was chosen because it captures a unique *snapshot* of our Vineyard DNA, and therefore represents a variety of authors and approaches.

In many chapters, we have also included personal reflections and stories from leaders around the world on various topics. These contributions personalize the material, add repetition of important ideas, and show how average people have been impacted by the Kingdom of God – and their experience of the Kingdom within the Vineyard Movement.

It is important to note that THE VINEYARD DNA does not attempt to comprehensively describe what makes the Vineyard a unique part of the Body of Christ in our time, nor does it attempt to give a full history or values statement for the global Vineyard family. There are many associations of Vineyard churches around the world, and there are nuances to all of them that would make that a complicated (and potentially inaccessible) project.

Rather, the goal of this book is to give you a "launch point" from which to understand and reflect on who the Vineyard is in the 21st century Church – what makes us tick. The unique genetic code that shapes how we partner with the Father in His work is a special gift to the Body of Christ and the world. And while we recognize that we are just one part of the beautiful, broader Church across history, we also celebrate the remarkable part we've had the privilege of playing in seeing renewal come to the Church in our time.

It has been said that if we don't know the story of where we came from, it is very difficult to know who we are now or where we are going in the future. This book seeks to define the basic, core identity markers of the Vineyard Movement, and to empower you and others looking to the future with hope for the world Jesus loves (Jn. 3:16).

The integration of young people and new people in the Vineyard creates a need both for ongoing education about the Vineyard, and for information revealing *why* the Vineyard has emerged as one of the most successful church planting movements of the 20th and 21st centuries.

There is much material that is available in well-written books about the Vineyard, and more resources are recommended at the end of this work. However, little exists that effectively *summarizes* the history, values, distinctives, and practices that make us who we are in the wide world of expressions of the Church. *THE VINEYARD DNA* attempts to be one of those summaries.

The book is designed to be read personally, but also to be effectively used as teaching content for small groups, staff training, and newcomer classes. *THE VINEYARD DNA* will encourage discussion on ideas central to the enduring impact of the Vineyard Movement, and we trust will provoke you to "seek first the Kingdom of God" (Matt. 6:33) in fresh and transforming ways.

We hope this collection serves you well into the future, as a Christian, and as someone who cares about the values and practices that make the Vineyard such a vital part of the Body of Christ today.

The Vineyard Resources Team

**"...To equip the saints
for the work of ministry...."**

EPHESIANS 4:12

CHAPTER 1
WHAT IS THE VINEYARD?

As we begin, let's answer a very simple question that will frame the rest of the content of this book: *"What is the Vineyard?"*

The Vineyard Movement is a *global community of churches* with a common heritage and set of values. We are organized in a fairly simple structure, but we are mainly held together by relationships. Most Vineyard churches were planted from other Vineyard churches, and meetings between pastors and leaders often have the feel of a family reunion.

Vineyard churches have a refreshing blend of unity and diversity. There are some qualities you will find at almost any Vineyard church: intimate worship, openness to the Holy Spirit, and a high value placed on relationship and community. At the same time, because we value the autonomy of the local church, there will be wide variations of church size, buildings, music styles, preaching styles, and any number of other features of a church body. We believe this diversity

THE VINEYARD DNA

is a strength, as it enables us to reach the many regions and people groups of the world with various forms and expressions of doing life together as Christians.

Vineyard Associations around the world have different types of leadership structures that support the diverse pastors and communities in their nation. The Vineyard in the US has some national structures that help hold the movement together – a national director and executive board provide leadership. Regular meetings at both local and national levels provide a place for community and care as well as broad vision-casting for all the different pastors and leaders in our movement.

Pioneering has always been part of the Vineyard's DNA, so many of our priorities are organized around launching new domestic and international congregations. We work together to identify places where God might be calling us, pinpoint leaders, and develop strategies to see new churches come into being.

Pioneering in worship has always been a central part of Vineyard churches. Perhaps over the years the most well-known arm of the Vineyard has been Vineyard Worship – with music coming from the US, UK, Canada, and around the world. Its leaders strive to find the best songs and approaches to leading congregations into heartfelt worship singing, and to document them for our movement and the wider Church.

Through albums, conferences, and training events, Vineyard Worship distributes these values to the rest of the Vineyard and beyond. Vineyard Worship historically has been one of the most impacting branches of the Vineyard both inside and outside our movement.

The Vineyard is committed to being a community of churches that live out the words and works of Jesus. But how did we get started, and who are we now?

OUR HISTORY

A Brief Snapshot

The first Vineyards were planted in the US in 1975. By 1982, there were at least seven Vineyards in a loose-knit fellowship of churches. Kenn Gulliksen, a soft-spoken, unassuming leader with a passion to know and walk with God, started a church in Hollywood in 1974. In 1975, believing that God had instructed him to do so, he officially gave the name "Vineyard" to this association of churches and led them for about five years.

In the early 1980s, Kenn felt led to ask John Wimber to assume leadership for the growing movement. The official recognition of this transition took place in 1982: the emergence of what was to be called the first Association of Vineyard Churches. There are now 13+ Vineyard Associations representing many countries worldwide.

John Wimber

John Wimber's influence profoundly shaped theology and practice of Vineyard churches, from their earliest days until his death in November 1997. When John was conscripted by God, he was, in the words of *Christianity Today*, a "beer-guzzling, drug-abusing pop musician, who was converted at the age of 29 while chain-smoking his way through a Quaker-led Bible study."

In John's first decade as a Christian, he led hundreds of people to Christ. By 1970 he was leading 11 Bible studies that included more than 500 people. John became so fruitful as an evangelical pastor he was asked to lead the Charles E. Fuller Institute of Evangelism and Church Growth in California.

He also later became an adjunct instructor at Fuller Theological Seminary, where his classes set attendance records. In 1977, John re-entered pastoral ministry to plant Calvary Chapel of Yorba Linda.

During this time, John's conservative evangelical paradigm for understanding the ministry of the church began to grow. George Eldon Ladd's theological writings on the Kingdom of God convinced John intellectually that all the biblical gifts of the Holy Spirit should be active in the Church.

Encounters with Fuller missiologists Donald McGavaran and C. Peter Wagner, along with seasoned missionaries and international students, gave John credible evidence for combining evangelism with healing and prophecy. As he became more convinced of God's desire to be active in the world through all the biblical gifts of the Spirit, John began to teach and train his church to imitate Jesus' full-orbed Kingdom ministry. He began to "do the stuff" of the Bible, about which he had formerly only read – and he led others to do the same.

Early Experiences With The Holy Spirit

As John and his congregation, mostly made up of former Quakers, sought God in intimate worship, they experienced empowerment by the Holy Spirit, significant renewal in the gifts of the Spirit, and conversion growth. Since it soon became clear that the church's emphasis on the experience of the Holy Spirit was not shared by some leaders in the Calvary Chapel movement, John's church left Calvary Chapel in 1982 and joined the Association of Vineyard Churches.

A Network Of Churches Worldwide

Over time, the Vineyard Movement has grown to be a network of over 2400+ churches worldwide. We seek to blend the best of the evangelical traditions with their focus on Christ-like character and regard for the Scriptures, with the best of the Pentecostal and Charismatic traditions of welcoming the empowering of the Holy Spirit for life, ministry, and acts of service.

That network of churches will continue to grow, as we are, at the very core, a church-planting movement. We work to extend the Kingdom of God by helping our local churches fulfill their God-given call to multiply, reproduce, and plant new churches.

A Church Planting Movement

As a movement, we actively work alongside our existing churches to help facilitate the multiplication of new Vineyard churches, who will in turn impact their local communities. We believe that the multiplication of local churches, in all their forms, is the most effective form of evangelism.

Here are just a few of the ways we further this church planting mandate within the Vineyard Movement.

1. We invest proactively in relationship with one another.

The Vineyard family is only as strong as our relationships with one another. As we intentionally work together to foster communication, respect, and affection, we are able to provide each other with the support, sharing of resources, and friendship that we all long for. Therefore, we highly encourage regular attendance at events and conferences to help develop and maintain relationships with other churches and leaders in the movement.

THE VINEYARD DNA

2. We partner with the Holy Spirit to innovatively multiply everything.
We believe that God is already at work in every Vineyard community around the world, and we seek to recognize and partner with the Holy Spirit in whatever the Father is doing.

Therefore, we embrace a diverse range of effective approaches to church multiplication, including classic church planting, multisites, missional communities, and other experiments in church multiplication – all in order to foster a culture of freedom, creativity, and risk-taking for multiplying churches.

3. We multiply churches out of existing healthy Vineyard churches.
A healthy local church effective in evangelism, discipleship, and leadership multiplication is the entity best suited to multiply a new church.

Because we reproduce what we know, we encourage church planters to be involved in a healthy local Vineyard church where they can embrace our core beliefs, come to understand and embody our values, and learn to live out the reality of our distinctives. We believe the local church is the best place to explore and discern a possible calling to lead in the body of Christ.

4. We respect and empower local leadership.
We work to support, encourage, envision, challenge, and resource our local pastors to multiply leaders and churches. Our local leaders know the areas where they minister the best, and have the closest relationships with the people they are training.

5. We equip pastors and leaders holistically in the context of our local churches.

Training new leaders is best accomplished in local Vineyard churches using the resources of our entire movement. We seek to equip these leaders in three large areas: knowing (theological education), being (life and spiritual formation), and doing (practical ministry experience). We expect these new leaders to engage in ministry in a local church before being released to lead on their own. This process enables us to discern together their calling and readiness to lead.

6. We encourage local churches to partner with each other to multiply churches.

Churches working together in partnership can accomplish what none of them could alone. We believe that every single Vineyard church can help birth new churches by partnering with other churches that share a vision for a particular target area. Partnerships make church multiplication available to churches of all sizes and ages. No church is expected to go it alone!

7. We trust God to provide the resources necessary to accomplish His vision.

God is faithful to supply where He guides. God has already given us the resources we need in order to be healthy, including financial and leadership resources. We can trust that He will give us what we need to do what He's called us to.

Our task is to be faithful with what God has given us. We want to foster creativity with the resources God has given us, believing we have what we need to accomplish what He's asked us to do.

THE VINEYARD DNA

A PERSONAL REFLECTION
Phil & Jan Strout

"There are a number of things that come to mind when we are asked 'What is the Vineyard?' We are going to attempt to express our thoughts in a very simple way, from our point of view.

The Vineyard is God's idea. We often refer to the Vineyard as a 'movement of people' that God initiated and invited, among many others, to join His mission. In other words, we are recipients of and participants in God's great grace and mercy.

We are a people who have responded to this invitation to join God's mission, for His greater glory and the well-being of people. In responding to the invitation of God, men and women like the Wimbers, the Fultons, and numerous others found themselves swept up in a Holy Spirit avalanche. These people who were at the beginning of this movement did not sit in a boardroom and draw up a five-part plan to form a movement that would spread around the world. This is very important for our present understanding of the Vineyard.

We were called into being as worshippers and Jesus-followers, grateful and humbled by God's inclusion of people like us. As we understood early on, we received much from God in relation to His presence – His power, His favor, His fruit. We all heard: 'We get, to give.' What God had done in the people of the Vineyard, He wanted to do through these people. We have not moved very far from that simple understanding, nor should we.

'Church, church, church!' John Wimber's clear instruction to 'Love the whole Church' was a refreshing and liberating invitation. Worship songs with lyrics such as 'Help me to love the things You love' (Danny Daniels)

reflected this emphasis. The Vineyard taught us all to not only appreciate, but also to embrace, the great historic traditions of the Church.

God has always had a people. Despite our penchant for viewing ourselves as innovators in the 21st century, we must realize that we aren't as vogue as we think. Instead of blazing trails with our faith, we have taken the torch that has been passed down to us from generation to generation. We are a family of torch-bearers.

'Find out what God is doing in your generation and fling yourself (recklessly) into it.' That is a paraphrase of a Jonathan Edwards quote that caught our attention during the Jesus Movement in the 70s. It is not that God changes, or that His message changes. Rather, it is often that a vital truth has been lost or disregarded – and it needs to be rediscovered, revived, and made alive again.

During the time of the birth of the Vineyard, the church was rediscovering the 'charismata,' or gifts of the Spirit. Incorporating them into the life of the church, with all of us participating ('everyone gets to play'), was one of the highlights of Vineyard understanding. Instead of the 'one' getting to play, 'everyone' was getting to play. There was no special person, no superstars. Even in our music, the simplicity of the chords and words took music that might have headed into performance back to intimacy, without hype.

First generation Vineyard people came from an incredibly varied set of backgrounds. We ranged from burned-out church leaders from many denominations, to those who had never set foot in a church building. Some showed up in suits and ties, only to find out that the casual mode (in dress and attitude) of the Vineyard atmosphere was actually an intentional piece of our liturgy.

THE VINEYARD DNA

In those days, the wide range of doctrinal statements was of little importance. We said, 'Come as you are, you'll be loved.' God was gathering a people made up of ordinary people.

The Vineyard Movement has a very unique opportunity to pass on a healthy template of what it means to be the Church to another generation. We will stay flexible and pliable in what is negotiable, as we stay the course in our main and plain, divine assignment to be worshippers of God and rescuers of people."

VINEYARD VALUES EMERGE

As the Vineyard Movement matured, a tension began to develop between preserving the historic DNA that had defined our movement and allowing congregations to innovate and develop relevant practices within their particular geographic locations or demographics.

When Vineyard leaders engaged this question there seemed to emerge a set of values in our history: central priorities of our movement that might be expressed in different ways but would always be part of what it means to be *Vineyard*.

The values can be introduced by the phrase, *"We are a people of the Kingdom of God who…."* This introduction is no mere window dressing. It emphasizes both the ordinariness and the extraordinariness of what God has called us to. We are a *people* first. Not an institution, not a government, not a force, but simply a people. And we are a people of the "Kingdom of God" – our central theological lens through which we understand the teaching of Jesus (Mk. 1:14-15).

We are a people seized by something beyond ourselves and turned into something new, something that is transformative to the world around us. Our values draw this reality out. Here is a summary of some of those values, to be explored more fully in a chapter 7.

We Are A People Of The Kingdom Of God Who...

Partner with the Holy Spirit. We are not simply implementing the best church strategies and trying to accomplish what is humanly possible. Rather, our mission involves praying and finding power from God Himself to accomplish what humans could never accomplish on their own. We pray for the sick; we confront injustice; we seek to hear the voice of God on behalf of others. This involves partnership with a Person beyond ourselves.

Experience and worship God. Worship has always been one of the calling cards of the Vineyard. Many people describe their first moment in the Vineyard as being the moment in which they encountered God through intimate worship singing. Worshipping and experiencing God goes far beyond singing. In every moment of our lives, we seek to live in the presence of the Lord. At the same time, corporate singing is a precious part of what it means for us to be the people of the Kingdom.

Reconcile people with God and all creation. The Bible tells the story of the Fall. This is the moment when humans rebelled against God and chose their own way over and against the will of God (Gen. 3:1-24). The result of the Fall is isolation and alienation. Self-centered creatures care more for themselves than they care about God, people, and His creation. The declaration of the Kingdom of God is an act of profound reconciliation: bringing people back to God, into deep relationship with each other, and into a life of caring about God's creation again.

THE VINEYARD DNA

Engage in compassionate ministry. There is a profound place in the story of Jesus in which a great crowd has gathered to see His ministry, the healings and miracles He did, and the profound wisdom He offered. It says that Jesus looked out at the crowd, He had compassion on them, and He commissioned his disciples to minister to them. Compassion is not about pitying people; rather, it is seeing people in their difficult, complicated life situations and believing that God is able to use His people to minister hope and healing to them.

Pursue culturally relevant mission in the world. Most people don't like change. Whether it's food, sports, music, or clothing, people tend to try to keep things the same. But the message of the Kingdom was intended by Jesus to extend from culture to culture and from generation to generation.

This means that while our core values and beliefs do not change, the form in which they are expressed will change, from one country to another and from one decade to the next. The Kingdom of God can be expressed through casualness or formality, rock music or hip-hop, big churches or house churches. The key for us is to stay true to the mission of God, and to let God show us how His glory can be expressed in each new context.

A PERSONAL REFLECTION
John Wimber quotes that helped shape our identity.

"The Kingdom is about doing just as much as teaching. If you aren't doing the works of the Kingdom the message isn't complete. I pray the Vineyard never stops taking the risks of the Kingdom."

"What I want to see in action is the message, the music, and the ministry. We must take the hype out of ministry – where everyone gets to play."

"The call of the Kingdom isn't just one part of our life; it's all of it!"

"The Vineyard is God's idea. He called us as Kingdom people, doing the stuff of proclamation and demonstration. To do only half of what we've been called into is not a complete Gospel message, and we must do all of what God's placed upon us."

"The manifestation of the Spirit is not supposed to be the exception – it's supposed to be the norm."

"The test of spiritual maturity is not the ability to speak in tongues, prophesy, or memorize Scripture. It's the ability to love God and others, learning to serve others by loving the unlovely, the less fortunate, the lost, and the broken. This is the highest call, that we would fulfill our purpose on earth."

"Ministry is a life of giving. We give our whole life, as God should have ownership of everything. Remember, whatever we give God control of, He can multiply and bless, not so we can amass goods, but so we can take an active part in His enterprise."

"You can't learn how to heal the sick by reading a book or mastering a technique. You believe what Jesus promised and then you get out and do it ."

"I've never been on a mission to make the Vineyard famous. It's not about the Vineyard. It's about Jesus. His fame is what our mission should be."

THE VINEYARD DNA

"It's not just about being biblically literate, we must also become biblically obedient."

"Power evangelism isn't about adding to the Gospel or seeking to add power, but rather turning to the Holy Spirit in our evangelistic efforts and consciously cooperating with His anointing, gifting and leading."

"Serving the poor isn't an option. If we don't care for the poor we're good as dead. I see it as a life and death matter."

"Faith is spelled R-I-S-K."

OUR UNIQUENESS

One book written about the Vineyard was called *The Quest For The Radical Middle*, by Bill Jackson. The idea put forward was that a healthy church movement is able to hold on to two sides of a tension, valuing both, without giving either up.

The Tensions We Embrace

There are a number of these tensions that describe some of the distinctives of our movement.

We are both Word-focused and work-focused. By "the Word," we mean the Bible. We are deeply committed to knowing, teaching, believing, and obeying the Bible. We believe in a God who reveals Himself, first through Jesus Himself and also through the words of Scripture. Scripture is how we find out who Jesus was and is.

And alongside the word of God, we are focused on the works of God.

John Wimber was famous for telling us "not to eat the menu," by which he meant that if a person reads the Bible but never does what it says, it will have no impact on that person's life.

We are both reverent and casual. If you go into any Vineyard church, it's likely you'll notice a casual feel. Vineyard folks like to wear jeans or shorts and bring coffee right into the service. Humor is often sprinkled throughout the message, and if there is a glitch in the service, usually no one is bothered and we move right on.

But this doesn't translate to being casual about God! Our casual style means we take ourselves less seriously, yet at the same time we take the Lord very seriously. It's not intended to take attention away from the Lord, but rather to take attention away from ourselves and put it on him.

We are both spiritual and non-religious. We believe deeply in spiritual realities. We regularly invite the Holy Spirit to be among us. We ask God to do things we could never do ourselves. We commit ourselves to prayer, Bible reading, confession, and other disciplines of faith.

And we are aware that all of these carry the danger of becoming empty religious acts with no real authentic faith behind them. We choose to live in this tension. Seeking Spirit power from the living God, we are always willing to acknowledge that we can slip out of true devotion into mere play-acting.

At our best, honoring our identity as people of the Spirit while being non-religious is a form of humility that marks our movement.

THE VINEYARD DNA

We are both intentional and spontaneous. The Vineyard Movement loves the spontaneous move of the Spirit. One of the most exciting parts of any Vineyard meeting is that you never quite know what is going to happen next. But we don't think there's any reason that our love for spontaneity has to be at odds with intentional, careful planning. Our God works both through unplanned moments of power and purposeful strategizing, when in a Sunday service, at work, in school – or anywhere at anytime.

A PERSONAL REFLECTION
Homero Garcia

"The key to being a successful tightrope walker is balance. Balance is a matter of life or death. The same applies to the Vineyard. I think the secret of its success is its balance.

If you were to ask me, 'What is the Vineyard?' I would have to say that the Vineyard is balance. It is balance between the evangelical movement and the charismatic and Pentecostal movements. It is balance between being Bible-based and Spirit-empowered.

It is balance between the already of the Kingdom of God and the not yet of the Kingdom of God. It is balance between following traditions and being relevant.

It is balance between letting God do His part in my life and in my church and me doing my part in my life and in my church. It is balance between being a movement and being an autonomous church.

It is balance between being released to be on your own and being held accountable. It is balance between my personal devotional life, my family life, my work life and my ministry life.

I love the Vineyard for its balance."

A PERSONAL REFLECTION
Jamie & Michelle Wilson

"Years ago, not long after the birth of our first child, I (Michelle) was asked to share my testimony at church on a Sunday morning. I was really nervous about speaking in front of people and also really excited to share about how Jesus had transformed my life.

I spent a long time planning exactly what I would say and shaping it around the Scriptures. I spoke at the first of our two services and felt good about how it went. Then, I was in for a surprise.

Our senior pastor, Don Williams, approached me during the worship time for our second service and invited me to expand on what I had said, taking the entire time designated for the sermon. When I stood up to speak, Don said, 'I'm not preaching this morning. Michelle Wilson is preaching!' I was shocked to hear him use those words, but I realized he was right – that what I had prepared was a sermon, and what I was doing was preaching.

One thing we have always loved about the Vineyard is the idea that 'everyone gets to play!' In the Vineyard we're committed to the belief that every follower of Jesus is given gifts from the Holy Spirit that are intended to be used to build up the ody of Christ. We are also committed to the practice of empowering every person to discover and use their own gifts.

THE VINEYARD DNA

For me (Jamie), my first steps in ministry were also surprising. When I was a year and a half sober, and only days after I finished my undergraduate education, Don asked me to take leadership of The Branch Ministry, the church's outreach to the poor and homeless.

I had been volunteering once a week in this ministry and had a growing sense of my call to serve Jesus, but I never expected to start full-time ministry at the age of 22. I didn't have any leadership experience, and I was still trying to figure out what following Jesus meant. Nevertheless, God had been showing me His heart for people living outside, and Don recognized gifting and calling in me and gave me a place on the field to play.

One of the reasons we're in the Vineyard today is because a pastor called out the gifts he saw the Holy Spirit growing in our lives and encouraged us to take a risk in using and developing those gifts. As we've grown up in our faith in the Vineyard community, we've met countless people, both those in vocational ministry and those who serve in the hours they have in between other commitments, with similar stories of being encouraged in their gifts and given a place on the team.

We've tried to carry on this tradition as pastors of our own church. We look forward to seeing a new generation of women and men from every ethnicity, young and old, using their gifts to serve Jesus and to bless the world!"

A PERSONAL REFLECTION
Adam Russell

"We are a people who have been awakened to the reality that God is not

nearly as far away as we once thought. He's near – He is always near! And it is His nearness that shapes everything we do and everything we are. I didn't grow up in the Vineyard, but I did come of age in the Vineyard. I was 17 when I went to my first Vineyard meeting. I remember being blown away by the worship, the pastor who didn't wear a suit, and the ministry time.

For years I couldn't articulate why those early experiences were so meaningful, but then one day I was telling a friend about the Vineyard when he summed it up perfectly: 'You really believe that God is in the room!'

In the Vineyard we believe that God is actually in the room. He's with us every single Sunday. Not only that: we are waking up to the fact that He is with us every day as well. It's why we mostly sing songs to God. It's why we pray for the sick and believe for the impossible. It's why we let everyone join in the work of the ministry.

God didn't come because a couple of morally superior, super-Christians happened to be in the room. No! We figured out that He loves people so much that He's present even when the room is filled with the least and the lost.

And He often shares his best gifts with the people everyone else has forgotten. We work for justice because God has brought His just Kingdom into our midst. We endure hardship and loss without losing heart because the crucified Christ is with us. We look for the lonely and the outcast because the Good Shepherd, who regularly leaves the 99 to go after the 1, shows up when we do the same.

The Vineyard is diverse. We are city, and we are country. We are rich, and

THE VINEYARD DNA

we are poor. We are Black and White and Latino and Asian, and all the complex mixtures of each. We are old school, and we are new school. We are Boomers, and Generation X, Y, and Z.

But most importantly, we are people who are awake to the nearness of God."

CHAPTER 2
WHAT IS THE KINGDOM OF GOD?

Now that we've looked briefly at the story of the Vineyard, we turn to the core teaching of Jesus that informs all that we believe and do as Christians – theology and practice of the *Kingdom of God*.

Why Theology Matters

For thousands of years Christians have studied the Bible to discover more about the God who is the central figure in its magnificent plot. What we think about God, and what we believe He is doing in the world, affects our everyday lives.

In fact, what we understand to be God's plan for the world, and His plan for each one of us, is a matter of ultimate importance to every human being who has ever lived. Knowing about God, and His purposes for the world, is what theology is really all about.

Theology is the study of God, or as one writer said, "Faith seeking understanding."

THE VINEYARD DNA

In other words, we want to know who God is, but we also want to *know* God in a vital and deepening relationship.

In the Vineyard, we look to the Scriptures – the Old and New Testaments – to guide our theology, and to teach us about the nature and purposes of God. We believe that God has self-revealed His character in the Scriptures, and nowhere more do we see Him self-revealed than in the life and teaching of Jesus (Heb. 1:3).

Jesus' Most Central Teaching

Learning to know Jesus, and to become like Him, is the goal of the Christian life. And if we truly want to be like Jesus, we must understand His most important, overarching, and integrating message about the world – His message of the Kingdom of God.

In Mark 1:14-15, we read these powerful words:

"... Jesus went into Galilee, proclaiming the good news of God. 'The time has come,' he said. 'The Kingdom of God has come near. Repent and believe the good news!'"

From the moment Jesus shows up on the scene in Israel, He begins to proclaim the reality of what He called the "Kingdom of God." Through stories and metaphors, miracles and healings, Jesus sends out one important declaration to anyone who will listen:

The Kingdom of God is breaking into this world – and it changes everything.

THE KINGDOM JESUS PREACHED

What Is A Kingdom?

To understand what Jesus meant by the phrase, "the Kingdom of God," we must first understand what a *kingdom* is. When we in the Western world hear the word, we may think of kings and queens ruling in empires like England. A regent over a kingdom is someone who has authority in that kingdom. That kingdom is a place where he or she actively rules and reigns.

So, what did it mean when Jesus said that God has a kingdom, and that it has come near?

What Is The Kingdom Of God?

The Kingdom of God, as Jesus spoke about it, was not limited to a physical city, country, or land mass – even to the borders of ancient Israel. Rather, the Kingdom of God was the dynamic reign of God over heaven and earth; all things visible and invisible.

For the ancient Jews, the idea of the "Kingdom of God" was an accepted theological reality. Taught by prophets like Isaiah, the people of Israel believed that God is the one true King and Creator of the world. As King, He rules the cosmos (Ps. 24:8-10), and will one day express that rule fully on earth through his selected regent – an anointed one (Is. 61:1).

On that day, God's people, Israel, will be delivered from their oppressors and brought home from their long exile. The world will be set to rights, brought under God's *shalom* (peace) again as it had been in the beginning. God's anointed, appointed King will rule the people of the world with justice, mercy, and love. This was the day for which they hoped, prayed, and persevered.

THE VINEYARD DNA

Jesus Inaugurates The Kingdom

Jesus, a simple carpenter's son and a Jew, is born in 1st century Palestine. One day, as a young man, He steps forward in a synagogue to read the Old Testament. He chooses a revered text that speaks of the anointed King to come. It is from the prophet Isaiah, chapter 61.

Here is the account:

"He stood up to read, and the scroll of the prophet Isaiah was handed to him. Unrolling it, he found the place where it is written: 'The Spirit of the Lord is on me, because he has anointed me to proclaim good news to the poor. He has sent me to proclaim freedom for the prisoners and recovery of sight for the blind, to set the oppressed free, to proclaim the year of the Lord's favor.' Then he rolled up the scroll, gave it back to the attendant and sat down. The eyes of everyone in the synagogue were fastened on him. He began by saying to them, 'Today this scripture is fulfilled in your hearing'" (Luke 4:17-20).

Jesus was declaring Himself to be the anointed King for whom they had been waiting! He would proclaim, in word and deed, that God's Kingdom was truly among them. He would demonstrate that Kingdom in signs, wonders, and the transformation of every life he touched. Then, by His death on a cross, He would offer himself as a sacrificial lamb, the "suffering servant," for the sins of all humanity (Is. 53).

By His resurrection from the dead (Luke 24:1-6), God would verify that Jesus was indeed the true King of the world. Jesus was inaugurating the rule and reign of God on the earth, and God's purposes for the world from creation would begin to be realized.

A PERSONAL REFLECTION
Rich Nathan

"One of the most challenging questions confronting Christian faith is simply this: If Jesus really was who He said He was, if He really was the long-awaited Jewish Messiah, then why is the world still in such bad shape? Why do so many people still die of hunger and cancer? Why are there still so many wars and suicide bombings? Why is there still so much slaughter taking place in Syria, in Iraq, and in Afghanistan? Why is rape used as a common tactic of war across the African continent?

Let me make this really simple. If Jesus is Lord and He has all power and we have the Holy Spirit, and we have this powerful message called the Gospel, then why aren't we more successful than we are?

Why are so many marriages, even among church-going, supposedly Bible-believing Christians, in such bad shape? And why do some Christian marriages end in divorce? Why do so many kids raised in Christian families end up barely connected to church? Why are so many church-goers living double lives, hopelessly addicted, unhappy, unfulfilled?

The bottom line is that if Jesus is really true and is really risen, why is the truth not more obvious? Why don't more people believe what Christians believe? Why is the world not in better shape if the Messiah really did come?

Haven't you wondered about this? Have these questions crossed your mind? For the last hundred or so years New Testament scholars have been unanimous in saying that the basic message of Jesus concerned the Kingdom of God. Jesus came preaching that through His person and His ministry the Kingdom of God had broken into the world. So we read lots

THE VINEYARD DNA

of texts like this one:

'After John was put in prison, Jesus went into Galilee, proclaiming the good news of God. "The time has come," he said. "The Kingdom of God has come near. Repent and believe the good news!"' (Mark 1:14–15).

So what is the Kingdom of God? What did Jesus mean when He said, "The Kingdom of God has come near?" Is He saying Christianity has come near in my person? Is the Kingdom of God the Christian religion? No. Is the Kingdom of God the church? Is Jesus saying the church has come near? Not at all. Is the Kingdom of God heaven? Not really.

What are we Christians praying when we pray in the Lord's Prayer, 'Thy Kingdom come, thy will be done on earth as it is in heaven?' Very simply, the Kingdom of God is what things would be like if Jesus ran everything and if His will was done everywhere. The Kingdom of God is what things would be like if Jesus was in charge.

When we pray 'your Kingdom come,' we are saying that we want this situation to be like what it would be like, if you, Lord, were in charge, if your will was done. We say the Kingdom has come when the Lord totally has His way, when He is running the show.

There is a secret that God has kept for all eternity, but has now disclosed. Everyone who listens to Jesus hears the secret that God's Kingdom is going to come in two stages. In the first stage the Kingdom is going to be hidden. It is not going to be obvious. You have to look for it and search for it. In the second stage God's Kingdom will be evident and open. It is going to be overwhelming, like a boulder from heaven.

In the first stage God's will doesn't displace every other will. In the first stage of the Kingdom coming into the world, God's will is done, but so is

36

the will of sinful human beings, and so is the will of Satan.

In the second stage of the coming of the Kingdom, when Christ returns, there will be only one will done on earth – the will of God. Right now, during this era, God's will doesn't always win the day. God's will can be resisted. God's will can be ignored.

The mystery of the Kingdom is that the Kingdom of God is here, but it hasn't replaced every other kingdom. The will of God is being done, but so is the will of sinful men and women, and so is the will of Satan. In this age, we're running on parallel tracks. When Christ returns creation is going to run on a monorail. Our world is going to run on the will of God."

THE NOW OF THE KINGDOM

God's Rule Breaks Into Our World

Through Jesus' life and ministry, God's future world – and its entire value system – was breaking into our human experience. Using a theological phrase, we call this *inaugurated eschatology*. Put simply, this means that Jesus inaugurated (ushered in) the gifts of God's future, perfect world (eschatology is about the "end" of the world).

God's future Kingdom, where healing and justice and love will reign supreme for eternity, was being brought into the present through the ministry of Jesus. In Jesus, humanity was experiencing the presence of God's future (George Ladd).

The Kingdom of God, God's rule and reign, was being established in hearts and lives as Jesus not only proclaimed the good news of God's plan to crush the works of Satan (1 Jn. 3:8), but also demonstrated that good news by healing the sick, casting out demons, offering radical forgiveness, extending compassion, and delivering the oppressed.

Every act of physical healing, every act of forgiveness, every action addressing poverty, is a foretaste of God's Kingdom that will come one day. God's Kingdom has broken into the world, is breaking into the world, and will break into the world one day.

Two Ways Of Talking About The Kingdom

As Jesus spoke about the Kingdom of God that He was demonstrating, He seemed to speak about it in two different ways.

The Kingdom of God, for Jesus, seemed to be both *now* and *not yet*. In other words, the Kingdom was something that was invading the earth through His ministry in the present. But then He would talk about the future Kingdom, when all wrongs would be made right, and He would reign forever and ever.

In the Vineyard we call this "living between the times." We as human beings live in the tension between the Kingdom revealed to us now, and the Kingdom that will be fully revealed at the end of time.

The Kingdom Now

What does it mean for God's Kingdom to come *now*? Wherever Jesus taught, signs and wonders followed him. Children were raised from the dead. Lepers were cleansed of their diseases. The lame walked. The blind were given sight. Multitudes were miraculously fed with small amounts of food. Prostitutes were shown mercy and kindness. Arrogant religious leaders were rebuked for their lack of compassion. The poor were treated with dignity as fellow image bearers of God

(Gen. 1:26-27). Women were afforded equal dignity with men. Compassion was shown to beggars, thieves, and drunkards.

The hand of God was touching the world through Jesus, and God was confirming Christ as His royal regent through signs, wonders, and miracles (Heb. 2:2b-4). He was a living, breathing revolution – and hearts were being changed everywhere.

Jesus Starts A Kingdom Apprenticeship

But it didn't stop there. Jesus then commissioned His disciples to do the same things that He was doing. They were going to proclaim, preach, and demonstrate God's rule and reign.

Working with their obedience, the Holy Spirit then extended the Kingdom into peoples' lives. Jesus never meant for the miracles to end with Him! This rag-tag band of fishermen, tax collectors, and Jewish laymen were participating with Jesus in the revealing of the Kingdom!

Every miracle, every act of justice and compassion, was pointing to the future day when God would completely set the world right again. The presence of the future was truly upon them – God's Kingdom had come near and the disciples were participating in the Lord's great restoration project.

In the Vineyard we believe that God acts in healing, power, and deliverance *today*. We also believe that the Kingdom apprenticeship Jesus began has never stopped – and is an invitation open to every Christ-follower, regardless of age, race, or background.

THE VINEYARD DNA

A PERSONAL REFLECTION
Derek Morphew

"By Kingdom theology I refer to an approach to the primary message and mission of Jesus as enacted, inaugurated eschatology.

This in turn forms part of the rediscovery of Jesus in the last century and this century that places him in the context of Second Temple Judaism. It can truly be said that since the discovery and translation of the literature of that period, Jesus research has been able to place Jesus in his historical context in a manner that was not possible in previous centuries. This rediscovery of Jesus is of major significance, since the way we see Jesus affects everything: the way we see God, salvation, mission, the Christian life, and the church.

The world into which Jesus came preaching the Kingdom had expectations that had grown through the centuries. These expectations were based on the coming of the Kingdom in the Exodus event, the conquest of the Promised Land and the Davidic Monarchy. They were further shaped by the loss of the Kingdom in the exile and the prophetic promises of Isaiah and Daniel in particular.

A day would come when God would again intervene for Israel, in a final, overwhelming moment, which would terminate history as we know it and begin life at a totally new level in the Messianic age, or the age to come. The Day of Judgment would be the event that would terminate this age (the end) and usher in the coming age. From the prophetic language regarding this 'end,' we derive the word 'eschatology' (the Greek eschatos means 'last'). The prophets spoke of the Day of the Lord, the last days, or that day.

Jesus came announcing that such a day had dawned with his arrival. Yet the way he announced and taught about the Kingdom had a sense of mystery. He spoke of it as being near, present, delayed, and future. The only way we can bring all of this together is to understand that something mysterious, unexpected (especially to the prophets of Israel) and miraculous occurred in Jesus and the outpouring of the Spirit at Pentecost.

The power of the future age broke through, from the future, into the present, setting up an altogether new dimension. Before this age has finally ended, the future age has already begun. The result is an 'already' and 'not yet' dimension, where the coming of the Kingdom in Jesus and Pentecost is 'already,' but in the final sense, the coming of the Kingdom is 'not yet.'

The mysterious breakthrough of the Kingdom was particularly manifest in the ministry of Jesus, as he announced it, taught about it and demonstrated it, in the cross, resurrection and ascension, and the outpouring of Pentecost. All these are demonstrations of the future breaking into the present.

Between the coming of the Kingdom in Jesus ('already') and the final coming of the Kingdom in Jesus ('not yet' – at his Second Coming) is the time we now live in as Christians and the church in the world. Around us is a world that lives in one dimension, in this present age, while we experience Jesus and the life in the Spirit in a new dimension, the life of the coming age, or eternal life lived now.

From this definition of the nature of the Kingdom, we have developed a set of initial implications:

THE VINEYARD DNA

1. The end has come in Jesus, therefore Jesus is God.

2. The last days begin with Jesus and Pentecost, and continue until the very end, so the whole period, from the first to the Second Coming, is the last days.

3. Every revival is a fresh in-breaking of the Kingdom.

4. Every part or aspect of the Kingdom is available every time it breaks through.

5. The veil torn when Jesus died shows that the separation of the present age and age to come has been torn, or opened up.

6. Therefore the powers and presence of the future age are continually available. We live in a dimension where it is always near, present, delayed, and future.

7. Church history bears witness to the increasing in-breaking of the Kingdom as we approach the end of the end.

8. This is the framework for understanding world missions.

9. This is the framework for understanding the Christian life, in the 'already' and 'not yet,' making us 'already ... not yet' people.

10. This is the framework for understanding healing, why it occurs, yet does not always occur.

11. This is the framework for understanding the church in the world."

THE NOW AND THE NOT YET OF THE KINGDOM

The Kingdom Not Yet

While the Kingdom of God was breaking into the world through Jesus, all human suffering, pain, and difficulty did not disappear. In fact, it still remains with us to this day. For Jesus, while the Kingdom of God was happening in the present, it was also yet to come in all its fullness in the future.

Through Jesus, God had inaugurated the Kingdom on earth, but He would consummate it one day in the future. In practical terms, this means that when we pray for the sick (a hallmark of the Vineyard from the beginning), some will be healed and others will not. Yet, with faith, we pray confidently for healing and entrust the results to God.

The Dynamic Tension We Live In

In the Vineyard, we embrace this dynamic tension. While we believe that God's Kingdom can invade any moment of our lives, not everyone will experience God's love the way we want for them. We rejoice when one person experiences a miracle of healing, while we grieve as another person succumbs to the effects of cancer or poverty.

Some Christians respond to this tension between the now and the not yet of the Kingdom by saying that God does not do miracles today. They contend that the gifts given by the Spirit of God were just for Jesus' time and are not available to us now.

Other Christians respond to this tension by largely ignoring the reality that suffering continues in the world. These groups triumphantly declare that the Kingdom should always be experienced demonstrably in the here and now – or something is *wrong*. If we don't experience physical healing or a significant personal transformation, it is probably our fault.

For them, unanswered prayer reveals a lack of faith in us – and we had better work up more if want to see God do what He has promised to do.

How We Carry This Tension In The Vineyard

In the Vineyard, we choose to respectfully step away from both of these extremes. John Wimber, the founder of the Vineyard, was well known for encouraging us to "love the whole church." While we do love the whole Church, we have certain values and practices related to our theology of the Kingdom of God that cause us to love being in the Vineyard Movement.

We believe that a necessary tension will always exist between the now and the not yet of the Kingdom. We pray for the sick, and we have seen many healed. We do the work of compassion, and we have seen the poor restored to hope. But we do not always see the results we want to see this side of heaven. Yet we believe that every faith-filled act of prayer puts a deposit of love in to the person who is suffering. And we have testimonies from every corner of the earth that, at times, the Kingdom of God does break through with power to heal those who are sick.

As we live in this interim time, the Kingdom of God to come is our future hope. It is a day when the Scriptures tell us that "all things will be made new" (Rev. 21:5) and every tear will be wiped away from the face of the brokenhearted (Rev. 21:4). It is the day Isaiah prophesied would come (Is. 35:1-10), and John describes in his vision in Revelation 21:1-5. There will be no more innocent children enslaved by the sex trafficking industry. There will be no more cancer. There will be an end to poverty. God will one day right this world.

Toward that day, we trust, we hope, and we pray in the way Jesus taught us to pray:

"Your Kingdom come, your will be done, on earth as it is in heaven" (Matt. 6:10).

A PERSONAL REFLECTION
Mark & Karen Fields

"What is the Kingdom of God? How might we experience it? Recently, in a conversation with a friend, he offered an interesting definition of the Kingdom of God, describing it as 'our world as God would have it.' Our personal ministry focus within the Vineyard is primarily international, and it is evident to us that the world is often not as God would have it. Far too often it is scarred by poverty, brokenness, and violence. The following story provides a glimpse into God's Kingdom work in our world.

Myriad storefronts and ramshackle dwellings, crowded with a cacophony of humanity, surrounded us as we wove our way through the rutted streets of Cebu City, Philippines, en route to the 'mission house.' We entered the concrete space, the ubiquitous white vinyl, stacking chairs lining the room in preparation for the morning service.

Filipinos, expats, missionaries, and visitors slowly congregated in friendly camaraderie, and soon began to sing in both English and Cebuano. We, both visitors and locals alike, were united in our shared experience of God's dynamic presence invading our gathering as we worshipped the Prince of Peace.

THE VINEYARD DNA

After lunch we visited a barangay named Lorega. This slum, only steps from the mission house, had long been distinguished by poverty and violence with, until recently, many of its residents building their homes in the graveyard. After a devastating fire three months earlier, its denizens were now rebuilding, although still living in crowded plywood shacks without running water, electricity, sanitation facilities, or gainful employment.

But what was truly surprising was to see so many familiar faces from church among its residents! Within the church community economic and social disparities weren't in evidence. The wealthy and the poor, the educated and the illiterate, the 'haves' and the 'have-nots' became one as we worshipped together – a paradigm of 'our world as God would have it!'

Walter Brueggemann's exposition on the Old Testament concept of shalom (peace) connects it with the New Testament teaching on the Kingdom of God expressed by Jesus in both His words and actions.

Jesus' ministry to the excluded (see Luke 4:16-21) was the same, the establishment of community between those who were excluded and those who had excluded them. His acts of healing the sick, forgiving the guilty, raising the dead, and feeding the hungry are all actions of reestablishing God's will for shalom in a world gone chaotic by callous self-seeking.

Shalom is about wholeness, prosperity, well-being, harmony, and goodness in the face of adversity. It is about when our world is as God would have it, everything is complete, all is as it should be, and nothing is missing. Our responsibility is to lean into shalom – the Kingdom in our own lives – and to align ourselves with God's work in the world.

As Brueggemann argues: 'Shalom in a special way is the task and burden of the well-off and the powerful. They are the ones held accountable for shalom' (Brueggemann, Living Toward A Vision: Biblical Reflections On Shalom, *p. 19)."*

HOW DO WE BECOME KINGDOM PEOPLE?

Christ's Rule & Reign

John Wimber had this to say about Jesus' Kingdom activity:

"... 'Kingdom' is translated from the New Testament Greek word *basileia,* which implies an exercise of kingly rule or reign rather than simply establishing a geographic realm over which a king rules. ...The Kingdom of God is the dynamic reign or rule of God. When Jesus said that the Kingdom of God had come in Him, He claimed for Himself the position of a divine invader, coming to set everything straight: 'The reason the Son of God appeared was to destroy the devil's works' (1 John 3:8)" (Wimber, *Kingdom Evangelism,* p. 12).

In other words, Jesus not only spoke words about the Kingdom – He went around Israel doing the works of the Kingdom. He was destroying the works of the evil one that bring physical and spiritual death to human beings.

Jesus had a message of Good News (that is what the word "Gospel" means), but He also had a ministry to back it up. As He trained His disciples, they became apprentices to His work, "doing the stuff " of the Kingdom of God.

THE VINEYARD DNA

In the Vineyard family of churches, we believe that Christians are commissioned and empowered by the Spirit of God to do the works of the Kingdom. With Jesus, we are empowered by the Spirit to bring "the presence of God's future" to our streets, neighborhoods, towns, and cities – in the hospitals, homes, and hearts to which He sends us.

Will you say "yes" to God – will you become a person who works with Jesus, in word and works, to demonstrate that the Kingdom of God is truly near?

A PERSONAL REFLECTION
John & Eleanor Mumford

"In her early thirties Eleanor had severe meningitis and was prayed for by some faithful Christian friends – and she was healed . . . instantly. The rule and the reign of the King, the reality of his Kingdom, had burst upon us! We immediately went back to the Bible, because my experience called for an explanation. And there we re-read the first recorded words Jesus spoke: 'The time has come, the Kingdom of God is near. Repent and believe the good news' (Mark 1:15).

This is momentous. Jesus Himself announcing Himself. The King proclaiming the Kingdom. Herein lies great drama. With the coming of Jesus, the King has arrived, and thus the Kingdom has come. But Jesus spoke of the Kingdom come and the Kingdom coming. The idea in Mark 1:15 is of the Kingdom almost here, about to arrive any minute. This is exciting and tantalizing, but it is also mysterious and – to be honest – (sometimes) frustrating.

This is the now and the not yet – the already and the not quite. Only when we grasp this reality does the explanation make sense, the experience resonate.

We had dinner only last night with people who were puzzling over why some people are healed and others are not. It was only as we began to talk about the Bible's understanding of the Kingdom, which we first heard articulated by John Wimber at his most groundbreaking, that any possible answers seemed to satisfy.

Over the centuries as the Church has struggled to understand this idea of the now and the not yet, the pendulum has swung from one extreme to the other. Some Christians have said all healing is available now and all the time, and unhelpfully have gone onto suggest that if you don't experience it, there's something wrong with you.

Other Christians, probably in reaction, have said 'no, no, it's not yet' and have pushed it all off to the future. But in the Vineyard we are convinced it's not either/or but both/and. The truth lies at both extremes. It's both 'now' and 'not yet.' And this makes sense to us. It explains why some people are dramatically healed by the power of God and others get sick and die. It explains why for every Peter who was released from prison by an angel, there was a James who languished and died there.

It explains Hebrews where we read of those heroes of the faith who conquered kingdoms, shut the mouths of lions, quenched the fire of the flames, escaped the edge of the sword. And yet in the very same verse (Hebrews 11:35) . . . 'Others were tortured, other faced jeers and flogging, others were chained and put in prison...put to death.'

Only our theology of the Kingdom of God can explain why some are carried from the field of battle shoulder-high, while others are dragged off...dead. Both the 'now' and the 'not yet' are realities and the tension in which we will always live this side of Heaven."

A PERSONAL REFLECTION
Bill Jackson

"The Kingdom of God is about all I think about now, but it wasn't always that way. When I used to read the phrase, 'the Kingdom of God' in the Bible, I always thought of the idea of a realm, like Camelot in the legend of King Arthur. Later, a seminary professor showed our class that while the Greek word, basilea (kingdom) can mean realm (e.g., Matt. 19.24), its primary usage in the first century was "reign" or "rule."

The professor then went on to show that when Jesus announced that the Kingdom of God was at hand, he was saying that God's rule, as King, had broken into the present age of evil to defeat the kingdom of Satan.

The Kingdom announcement, therefore, signaled the renewing of creation. After the sacrifice of Jesus' death, his resurrection to new life, and his ascension to God's right hand, he poured out the Spirit upon the people of God.

Through these events the end of the age had arrived. Like the climber who reaches the top of Mt. Everest and plants a flag for cause or country, in Christ, God was planting his flag and declaring, "THE UNIVERSE IS MINE!"

When Jesus told his disciples to do what he had been doing, to announce the Kingdom, heal the sick and cast out demons, this declaration and accompanying signs were evidence that the future had broken into the *present. In the words of another professor, Jesus came to bring his people back from exile to bring the world back to rights; salvation was not only for the whole person but also for creation itself.*

Yet the Kingdom has only just begun. As in Jesus' day, we still see rampant evil all around us. The road to salvation is narrow and it often seems that Satan has the upper hand – but not so with those who have put their faith in the one who has defeated all demonic powers.

While God's people must learn that suffering will be with us until the return of Christ, the Kingdom of God advances through pain as well as power. Kingdom warriors remain undaunted by defeat because in Christ, God rules as King. He is most glorified when the Church of Christ advances the Kingdom in the midst of sorrow.

In a small group recently someone received a word from God that there was someone there that had weak legs. I have peripheral neuropathy in my feet and it has been slowly moving up my legs. It is a very painful and potentially crippling condition. I have probably received prayer for it over 400 times. Why do I keep getting prayer? Because the Kingdom of God has broken in through Christ!

God loves me and loves you. His sovereign rule could burst in any minute to break the power of Satan, sickness, and the unjust systems over us. In this mindset I got up and received prayer for the 401st time. The next morning, while I still felt nerve damage in my feet, I had feeling in my legs for the first time in two years.

That's the already and not yet of the Kingdom of God. Believe and never give up. Jesus said, 'The Kingdom of God is at hand.'

Let us 'Repent and believe the good news!'"

THE VINEYARD DNA

CHAPTER 3
EVERYONE GETS TO PLAY

Theology of the Kingdom of God taught by Jesus seems to welcome every Christian into a vital way of living that is characterized by a full participation in the work the Father is doing! And the best part is that God plays no favorites – every person, no matter who they are, what age they are, or where they are from – gets to join in the fun.

Believing & Doing
Is being a Christian about believing the right things, or living a new way?

One of the weaknesses of the Church in the 20th century was the direct result of what scholars call *modernism*. Modernism was based on the idea that if we just gave people the right ideas, the right knowledge, they would then have happy and satisfied lives.

THE VINEYARD DNA

In the 21st century, we are coming to terms with the emptiness of this argument. Simply having intellectual knowledge does not lead people to live meaningful, satisfying lives.

John Wimber, the spiritual father of the Vineyard Movement, intuitively understood that much of the Church had given in to this error of modernism. That is, they were more concerned with telling people what to *believe* than showing them how to *live*.

There's a famous anecdote about Wimber going to church for the first time after coming to faith in his friend's living room. After a fairly dry sermon and singing time, he asked his friend, "When do we get to do the stuff? The stuff in that book? I gave up drugs for this?"

This intuition goes to the heart of one of the most important distinctives of the Vineyard: that we are a movement of people who want to learn to live like Jesus lived, not simply believe what Jesus believed. And we don't want this limited to the professional clergy — we believe that anyone can learn to live the kind of life that Jesus did.

The phrase that has come to embody this value in the Vineyard is the phrase *everyone gets to play* – which is another way of saying that the Holy Spirit can empower *anyone* to do what Jesus did.

WHAT DID JESUS DO?

Jesus' Way Of Leading

The life of Jesus of Nazareth is recorded in the four canonical books we call the Gospels. Each tells the story from a different angle, and the books fit together to paint a striking image of the man Christians believe was simultaneously human and divine. Thus there are aspects of His life that we can never emulate – His moral perfection, His perfectly clear wisdom, His redemptive death. And there are also aspects of His life that, through the empowerment of the Spirit, we can seek to emulate. So, focusing on those parts of His life we can pursue ... what did Jesus do?

First of all, Jesus welcomed. His welcome was as broad as the people He encountered. He was not a power broker; He was not strategically (or cynically) "networking" so as to maximize His potential influence. He did not see any one person as more righteous or valuable than another. Rather, Jesus' welcome was total. He hung out with people, especially with the marginalized. He loved to be with the poor and the outsiders. He liked to be with prostitutes and drinkers, doubters and thieves. These people found in Jesus someone who saw past their flaws to their inner person — the core part that the God whom Jesus called Father had created in His own image.

Second, Jesus healed. He healed the sick in every way imaginable. He brought sight to the blind, hearing to the deaf, life to the dead. He made people walk again, speak again, feel again. And He brought spiritual healing. To those oppressed by evil spirits, to those who were manic or depressed, to those whose inner demons had led them to isolation and alienation, He brought remarkable freedom. There is scarcely any clearer New Testament witness to any other aspect about Jesus than that He was a *healer*.

Third, Jesus summoned. His call was for people to repent and to follow Him. He welcomed and healed anyone, but He did not invite them to stay in their painful lives — He called them to change. He gave them hope that there was a different way of life available. He taught them what spiritual power without religious oppression looked like. He showed people what it meant to be convicted by God without feeling condemned. Jesus was remarkable in His spiritual genius, which could draw people to transformation without Him having to exert pressure or power.

Fourth, Jesus commissioned. The Gospels are replete with language about how Jesus' ministry, while in some ways utterly unique, was in other ways definitively intended to be *imitated*. His final words in the gospel of Matthew were "Go and make disciples of all the nations, baptizing them in the name of the Father and the Son and the Holy Spirit. Teach these new disciples to obey all the commands I have given you" (Matt. 28:19). This was not a religion for a single cultural moment.

Rather, Jesus intended to launch a global movement of the Kingdom of God – bringing life and hope to all people.

A PERSONAL REFLECTION
Rick & Becky Olmstead

"When we say 'everyone gets to play' we sometimes overlook youth, and we usually aren't referring to the kids in our churches. At best, we let them be spectators as we participate in the ministry of Jesus. But, Jesus told us, 'Let the children come to me, and do not hinder them, for the Kingdom of God belongs to such as these" (Mark 10:14b).

Is it possible for a child to be used by God to deliver a prophetic word? I heard of an instance just recently where a child told her mother, 'One, two, three, four... that's how many there are of us. But one is missing. He'll be here soon.' She was telling her mom that their family wasn't complete.

They would have one more brother. Within two years that brother was born.

Could a child speak a word of wisdom to an adult? A single mom who had angry blowouts with her children came to see me one day because her three-year-old daughter told her the night before, following an emotional outbreak, 'Mommy, Jesus doesn't like it when you treat us that way. Ask Him and He will help you change.'

Could a child's prayer bring healing? A four-year-old child prayed 'Jesus heal cancer' for a woman diagnosed with breast cancer. After a trip back to the doctor she learned that she no longer had a cancerous mass in her breast.

What if a child started a 'God talk' with his or her friends? Several kids from our church have. They have shared Jesus with their friends on the playground at school. One of our teenagers started a 'God talk' with a homeless man one very cold winter night. He ended up buying that man dinner, bringing him into his warm truck and praying for his foot condition, and then, rather than turning him out to sleep in the cold, he took the man home for the night. (The next morning his parents were very surprised.) Now that sounds like something Jesus would do!

We know that the Holy Spirit has distributed His gifts to all believers. Does it matter that a significant portion of believers are kids and teens? After all, one out of every four people in the world today is 14 or under. Could we be missing out on 25% of the ways God would like to see His Kingdom advance because we have overlooked including a whole population of youth when we say that 'everyone gets to play?'"

THE VINEYARD DNA

WHO DID JESUS COMMISSION TO DO KINGDOM WORK?

Jesus Taught A Way Of Life To His Disciples
The ability to do what Jesus did was never something that happened to people in some kind of instant spiritual download. Jesus taught a way of life, of intimacy with the Father and empowerment by the Spirit, that issued out into Kingdom living and could be passed on to the next generation.

Jesus had three close friends named Peter, James, and John. They spent more time with Him than anyone else did, and they all played significant roles of leadership in the early days of the Church. Then Jesus had another wider circle of 12 friends, including the first three, that have been known as *disciples* or *apostles*. He often withdrew from public ministry to spend time teaching, mentoring, and developing these leaders. They were a motley group from various walks of life and social spaces.

Extending The Ministry Of Jesus
Jesus' commissioning was not limited to His closest three friends, or only to the disciples. Some biblical passages talk about a group of 72 people that He commissioned and empowered to be ministers of the Kingdom. Other passages mention larger groups of "followers" who also seem to have been commissioned not only to experience the ministry of the Kingdom, but also to extend this ministry.

After the death and resurrection of Jesus, we are told a group of 120 believers obeyed Jesus' instructions to wait for the Holy Spirit to empower them for further ministry. The remainder of the New Testament makes it clear that very quickly, thousands more were commissioned with the power of the Spirit. Jesus had promised this would happen: "You will receive power when the Holy Spirit comes upon you. And you will be my witnesses, telling people about me everywhere – in Jerusalem, throughout Judea, in Samaria, and to the ends of the earth" (Acts 1:8).

On the day of Pentecost, thousands were baptized into the ministry of Jesus. Churches began springing up all over the Roman empire – in Ephesus, Colossae, Antioch, and even the imperial capital of Rome. Among Jews and Gentiles, men and women, poor and rich, educated and uneducated, people came to faith in Christ and discovered through the Holy Spirit the empowerment to do the same Kingdom works as Jesus.

The Church Is Not Always Perfect

2,000 years later, we have a rich record of how the Church has expanded all over the globe through everyday people being empowered to extend the Kingdom of God. Of course, it hasn't always been pretty. Jesus promised that one day He would return and bring the Kingdom in all its fullness.

Until that day, we experience the Kingdom of God as an *already and not yet* reality.

We have stories of God using His people to bring healing, salvation, and hope down through the generations. We also have stories of the Church being corrupt and hijacked by the powers of the day. People of faith mourn the *not yet* moments of the Kingdom, but believe that God still has hope for the Church to be the community of power and love Jesus meant for it to be.

THE VINEYARD DNA

A PERSONAL REFLECTION
Christian Dunn

"Wouldn't it be weird if we went to a high school football game, and instead of student athletes playing, only the coaching staff played while the students watched from the sideline? Every game, the coaches would sit the students down and say, 'Watch us! This is how you do it. And when you get older you can try it too, but not now. But trust us, it's awesome!'

A renewed emphasis on creating opportunities for teens and young adults to 'get to play' has been moving through the Vineyard. I believe this is absolutely crucial for the future of the Vineyard. And it is a strong focus in my own heart.

Working alongside teens and young adults has been incredibly gratifying for me. I find that they are a deep well of energy, talent, giftedness, vision, honesty, and creativity. I believe the time is now to harness this amazing resource that God has given to our movement!

But, it isn't going to happen magically. We adults need to proactively plan for and create meaningful ministry opportunities for our young people.

Why is this so important? Here are a few reasons I'd like to suggest:

1. Teens and young adults need their own 'God stories.'

As adults we know the impact our God stories have had on our lives. The question is – are we creating space for teens and young adults in the Vineyard to have their own experiences in ministry?

2. Tangible lessons last!

I don't remember many of the Bible studies I attended as a teen, but I do have vivid memories of the times where I prayed for people, saw healings, and shared my faith!

3. Our churches need young people in ministry now!

We simply can't wait. What they have to offer now will greatly benefit you, your church, and the community your church is reaching. Plus, they probably won't be around in 10 years if we don't give them a place now!

How can we make this shift? To start, teens and young adults should be trained, equipped, and released to minister in our churches much like adults are. We should have qualified teens on our worship teams, doing prayer ministry, praying for the sick, running service projects and outreaches, leading small groups, praying prophetically, speaking in front of the church, working behind the scenes administratively, and more!

The awesome piece is that this isn't a 'replacement' of adults. It is a partnership. I love to see adults and teens working together. There is so much value in adults sowing into the lives of young people. And, honestly, there is a ton of blessing for adults working with young people too.

So I encourage you! Ask the Lord how you and your church can create meaningful space for your young people. Let's welcome teens into the adventure of living naturally supernatural lives. Let's encourage them to experience the power and presence of God. Let's create space for them to play too!"

THE VINEYARD DNA

WHAT DOES IT MEAN FOR ME?

You Get To Play

Jesus commissions anyone who wants commissioning. His Kingdom ministry is for everyone; there are no disqualifications. Regardless of your personality, your history, or your gifting, Jesus wants to involve you in His plan for the world.

A group of teenagers and early 20-somethings gathered in a living room, led by a not-much-older couple in the late 1990s in suburban Chicago. Most of them had some kind of faith background but found themselves jaded and skeptical about religion.

But over the weeks, the wife of the not-much-older couple would play her guitar and sing simple songs of love to Jesus. The husband would teach simple, helpful truths from Scripture. And then they would take time to lay hands on each other and pray for the presence of the Spirit.

Person after person in that group would find themselves unexpectedly touched by the presence of God. Sometimes a sickness would be healed, but most often, they would simply find hardness in their hearts softened into love for Jesus. They often found themselves emboldened to do ministry.

Some would head to the mall to share Christ. Some felt called to overseas ministry. Some of them became lay leaders in local churches, leading small groups that cared deeply about reaching those around them. Others became pastors or missionaries or leaders of faith communities on college campuses.

People Empowered By The Spirit

This pattern repeats itself again and again throughout the Vineyard, and we believe it is simply a continuation of what Jesus was doing with His three close friends, His twelve disciples, and many beyond that. This is why it's impossible to stop the movement of Jesus through persecution, political oppression, or legal action.

The movement of Jesus does not depend on institutional support – it happens organically through people empowering other people in the power of the Holy Spirit in the same way they themselves were empowered.

A PERSONAL REFLECTION
Rose Swetman

"From the little boy who shared his lunch that fed over 5000 people, to the woman at the well whose story impacted an entire village, to a young Jewish girl in first century Palestine who said 'yes' to God and gave birth to Jesus, we know it's true: 'everyone gets to play.'

When we read through the pages of Scripture, we learn quickly that God's story unfolds throughout human history and is on a trajectory that has a goal: the redemption of the heavens and earth. Within the story, we see over and over again how God invites, commissions, and empowers broken humanity to join with Him in bringing forth His eternal purposes.

Some time ago several of our young people spent a weekend at an event called, 'City Serve.' They joined with hundreds of young people around the city and served in homeless teen shelters, gardening in community gardens, and the like. They prayed together, worshipped together, and had an amazing time playing in God's Kingdom.

Another time I had a conversation with an 80-something-year-old woman in our church that listens to so many folks within and beyond our church, and very often in her listening, God sends the one she is listening to a 'gracelet' specifically created for that occasion. I could tell you countless stories of people from every life stage that are participating in God's Kingdom work as they go about their everyday lives. Whether it is feeding hungry people, praying for the sick, or working in a community garden, everyone has something to bring to God's table that will be food for another's life.

Our worship gatherings are times where we can look for ways to create space for God to send His gracelets through and to His people, by encouraging young and old alike to listen to the Spirit of God and to be postured openly to be conduits of his gracelets. Training all ages how to minister with grace, love, and wisdom is a regular way of fostering a culture that brings heaven to earth. Some have said that the practices of the Vineyard are more 'caught than taught.' Creating spaces for people of all ages to continue the ministry of Jesus is how the church of today continues being a vibrant church for tomorrow.

During one of our Northwest region's biannual conferences, our tagline was 'every1gets2play.' From the youngest child to the elders among us, everyone had an opportunity to play: children praying for people of all ages, youth serving in a variety of ways throughout the conference, and adults teaching, praying, and singing.

It is a beautiful picture of God's people when we actively pursue folks in all walks of life to deliver His gracelets and use their talents for the sake of the church and the world."

EVERYONE GETS IN ON THE PARTY

So, how can you experience commissioning from Jesus? It's really worth the effort. No two people experience this commissioning in the same way. Jesus is our creator and knows our hearts better than anyone else. He formed us with a particular destiny: to carry on the work of His Kingdom in the midst of a complicated, difficult world.

Here are three steps to start on this journey:

First, look for some people who are experiencing Jesus' call in a way that is compelling to you. Go be around them. Watch how they live. They'll never be perfect (remember the "already-not yet" concept?). Don't let their imperfections disillusion you. But when they are at their best, pay attention. Ask questions.

Second, ask for them to show you how to "do the stuff." Ask to pray for the sick with them. Ask to serve alongside them in church or in the community. Ask if you can try leading for a week in the group they are heading up. You'll find that Jesus' people are typically pretty enthusiastic to show others how to do what they're doing. If you pursue some who aren't, move on until you find some who really want to include you.

Third, be ready to give it all away. It's surprising how quickly Jesus can turn us from trainees into trainers. Be on the lookout for people you can help grow into the destiny that Jesus has for them. You'll be amazed at how ready God is to empower the next group of people to do His Kingdom ministry.

Don't expect your Jesus-ministry to look like anyone else's. Everyone gets to play, and we all have a different part. We all have vocations, or callings, that are meaningful to God and reveal His heart to the world in a special way. Whether we join God's Kingdom work in our workplaces or neighborhoods, we can engage with what God is doing in those unique environments. The beauty of the Kingdom is that everyone has their own roles, and it can all come together to reveal the beauty of what God is doing in the world – and what He will one day bring to completion.

A PERSONAL REFLECTION
Jay Pathak

"Have you ever wanted to be a super hero? Flying through the sky, wind blowing in your hair, bending steel bars in your hands – admired by everyone and feared by your enemies? Maybe you weren't into comic book characters. Maybe rock musicians are your cup of tea. Or the walls of your room were covered with sports heroes. We all have someone that we look up to and admire. We admire them because we believe that they are different than us, and with some of our heroes, they seem unreachable.

In churches that believe in the power and the presence of the Holy Spirit, and want to see the kinds of miracles we see Jesus and the apostles doing, we create a whole different kind of superhero. We stand in rapt awe watching the 'man of God' on the platform delivering prophetic words proclaiming healing into the microphone. They exude such confidence and charisma, they seem far removed from the petty doubts and fears that normal people experience. They have stories that amaze and power that is obviously from God himself.

Just like the gifted athletes we watch on television, we begin to watch these leaders with awe and admiration. The more we watch them, the more convinced we are of their other-worldliness. We are more convinced with every moment that what they do they do easily – and we should never even attempt to try.

This is where I think the Vineyard has shown another way. The phrase that John Wimber was known to say often was 'everyone gets to play.' His goal was to create opportunities for normal people to do extraordinary things. The action wasn't always on the stage, but all around the room. In those Vineyard meetings he would give opportunities for people to learn how to pray for one another and begin discerning how to hear God's voice.

As that practice built confidence, faith would spill out of the room, traveling everywhere those people went. The goal of the Vineyard has always been to 'equip the saints for the work of ministry' (Eph. 4:12a). To train ordinary people to do extraordinary things – that has always been the idea behind the calling of the Vineyard movement in the world.

That sense of confidence and faith must have been the same feeling that the 72 felt after being sent out by Jesus (Lk. 10). These ordinary men and women came back amazed at what God had done through them. They couldn't believe that it worked. The sick were healed, and even the demons submitted when they prayed in Jesus' name. And Jesus' response to their excitement? Joy. Pure joy.

I bet He still feels the same way. He loves watching normal people do extraordinary things in the power of His name. Everyone gets to play."

CHAPTER 4
COME, HOLY SPIRIT

Sometimes, the simplest prayers are the best prayers. One prayer that has been prayed by the Church in many forms over the past 2000 years has become very important to us in the Vineyard family of churches.

It is the prayer "Come, Holy Spirit."

Mother's Day 1980
On Mother's Day, 1980, John Wimber had a unique experience at the church he pastored in Yorba Linda, California. John was from a Quaker tradition, and was a respected voice teaching leaders about church growth through evangelism.

John had invited a guest speaker named Lonnie Frisbee to teach at their evening service. Lonnie was a hippie who was a part of what became known as the Jesus People Movement in the late 1960s in Southern California. John's church was filled with young people, and they gathered to worship as usual that night. Lonnie got up to speak, and at the conclusion of his message he prayed a prayer that has been prayed by many throughout church history.

It was a simple prayer, one that has become one of the most important prayers we pray across the Vineyard family of churches. The prayer was simply:

"Come, Holy Spirit."

That night, when that three-word prayer was prayed, all heaven broke loose in John Wimber's community. An entire movement of churches has, in many ways, grown around that prayer. After that gathering, deeply encountered by the Holy Spirit, young people poured into the streets, leading hundreds, then thousands, to faith in Jesus Christ. Miracles followed their simple prayers, such as healings of bodies and minds, as well as deliverances from addictions.

Since that time, tens of thousands have come to faith in Jesus through the work of the Vineyard. Our belief in "Power Evangelism" – reaching people by participating with God in the miraculous – centers us on the Holy Spirit's work in drawing the heart to God.

Today, you will hear this simple prayer, in some form, being prayed in virtually every Vineyard church around the world. It is because we are learning in the Vineyard what the Body of Christ has had to learn again and again throughout history – that with the power of the Holy Spirit at work within us, we can do the works of Jesus. We can join Him in the advancing of the Kingdom of God to the ends of the earth.

THE VINEYARD DNA

We are a people of the presence of God. So we pray "Come, Holy Spirit."

THE THIRD PERSON OF THE TRINITY

Who Is The Holy Spirit?

Who is the Holy Spirit? In many churches you will hear messages on God as Father, and God as the Son. But how often will you hear a message about God as the Holy Spirit? The truth is that the Holy Spirit may be the least understood Person of what church history calls the Trinity – God the Father, God the Son, and God the Holy Spirit.

The Vineyard story is driven by the reality that God eagerly desires us to experience His presence. The presence of God is expressed by the Spirit of God, and it is the experience of the presence of God that empowers us to do the work Jesus has called us to do in the world.

Recognizing The Person Of The Spirit

We are committed to being functionally Trinitarian in all our church activities, recognizing that the presence of the Holy Spirit among us means everything to the church Jesus is building.

Recognizing the work of the Holy Spirit in our lives and communities, we are softened in our desire to become "change [coins] in God's pocket" (John Wimber) – people ready to be spent by the Lord and led by the Spirit into any act of Kingdom service He desires.

According to church history, the Holy Spirit is God, and as such, shapes our lives as God indwells us, by His Spirit through the work of Christ (Col. 1:27). In the Bible, the Holy Spirit is called by many names including the Comforter (Jn. 14:26), the Advocate (Jn. 14:16), and the Spirit of God (Gen. 1:2).

The Spirit is given to us as a deposit guaranteeing God's goodness to come (2 Cor. 5:5), to assure us of Christ's presence within (1 Jn. 4:13), to speak through us to one another (1 Cor. 12:18), to guide us in our understanding of God's gifts to us (1 Cor. 2:12), to empower us to impact nonbelievers (Mk. 1:11), and to give us rest (Is. 63:14).

Jesus And The Spirit
It is by the power of the Spirit of God that Jesus ministered:

"One day Jesus was teaching, and Pharisees and teachers of the law were sitting there. They had come from every village of Galilee and from Judea and Jerusalem. And the power of the Lord was with Jesus to heal the sick" (Luke 5:17).

The Spirit also empowered Paul and the other disciples to do the works of Jesus, and touched those to whom they ministered:

"As I began to speak, the Holy Spirit came on them as he had come on us at the beginning. Then I remembered what the Lord had said: 'John baptized with water, but you will be baptized with the Holy Spirit.' So if God gave them the same gift he gave us who believed in the Lord Jesus Christ, who was I to think that I could stand in God's way?" (Acts 11:15-17).

In the Vineyard we believe that the Holy Spirit, likewise, distributes gifts among us, His Church today. These gifts of healing, prophecy, prayer languages, miracles, and many other gifts enable us to experience God's presence personally and corporately.

THE VINEYARD DNA

These gifts enable us to minister to the world around us imbued with the power of God. In the Vineyard we believe that doing God's work in our own strength will burn us out – but doing God's work in His strength will fill us up.

A PERSONAL REFLECTION
Steve & Cindy Nicholson

"'Come, Holy Spirit.' We remember the first time those words were used by us as a conscious invitation to the Spirit to come, with an expectation that we might see evidences of the Spirit's presence. It was at our young church's annual dinner-come-slide-show-come-worship celebration. Everyone was standing. There was a deep, unnerving, very long silence.

Then in the cavernous acoustics of a church gym, the sound of a metal folding chair flipping over and the unmistakable wail of a man whose emotional pain had just gotten uncorked by God. More flipping chairs, more crying, laughing, shouting, people shaking, people ending up under folding chairs, and all through the room, such a sense of purposefulness to it all, of God doing things and saying things, as though we had finally opened the door and let Him in. Which we had!

'Come, Holy Spirit' did not originate with John Wimber. We are merely the latest generation to embrace it. It has its roots back in the earliest prayers of the first Church Fathers and Mothers, the first generation after the apostles to carry the flame of the gospel forward. This prayer is not just some oddity of 21st century Western Christianity. It is part and parcel of Trinitarian theology, a beloved prayer of every generation of believers before us. You are in very good company when you pray, 'Come, Holy Spirit.'

'Come, Holy Spirit' is a direct, bold request for the Spirit to do the work the Father wants to do in us, and to be the fire that propels us out to do the work the Father wants to do through us. The words are not magic (Oh, how many times have we found that out the hard way!); we have to actually expect the Spirit to accept our invitation! Otherwise it's a bit like standing inside our home saying 'Come on in!' to someone standing outside, but never actually opening the door.

'Come, Holy Spirit' is a prayer best prayed with willingness to welcome surprise and unpredictability. When we pray this prayer, we never know what will happen next! Most of us love the image of Aslan, in the C.S. Lewis Narnia books, as good but not tame. It's another thing entirely to be met by this not-tame Holy Spirit in real life! But nothing beats the joy of seeing the Spirit come and do what we are powerless to do in our own strength.

Go ahead – pray this prayer. Your life will never be dull again."

ALLOWING GOD TO ACT IN OUR MIDST

Learning To Live By The Spirit

Because the Holy Spirit is active in speaking to His people, to His Church, and to the world He loves all around us, our job as Christians is to give the Holy Spirit permission to move in our lives and gatherings. This is the first step in learning to live "life in the Spirit" (Gal 5:16-25).

The apostle Paul, in writing these words in the book of Galatians, is reminding the Church that the coming of the Spirit is the coming of God's presence to His people. To live "in the Spirit" is to live aware of God's presence – at all times, in all places.

THE VINEYARD DNA

The Bible also says that when we are aware of, and responsive to, God's presence in our lives, He will begin to change us from the inside out. As the Spirit shows us the love of the Father, we learn to serve the Spirit of God rather than our own cravings and desires. Powerful drives within us toward money, sex, and power are put in their proper perspective by the Spirit of God as we learn how to walk in love, joy, peace, patience, kindness, goodness, faithfulness, gentleness, and self-control (Gal. 5:22-23).

In the Vineyard we believe that God works often from the inside out, not demanding new moral character over night, but rather gripping our hearts and changing our desires to His own. For this reason, we create ample space in our gatherings for the Spirit of God to speak to individuals – and to change us in ways we cannot change ourselves.

Creating Space For The Spirit

Our corporate worship experiences seek to create an intimate place of encounter with God where His Spirit can touch us and speak to us. We are not in a rush trying to perform before God to get Him to respond; we value the moments where the Spirit is speaking to us because we are creating a space in which we can hear His voice.

This means that in what we call "ministry times," or times of prayer for one another, we seek to cultivate a listening posture before we speak. This kind of praying that begins by first listening to what the Spirit might be saying (rather than just praying our best wishes for the person) has resulted in some incredible stories over the history of our movement.

Catalyzed by times of Spirit-led, non-hyped prayer ministry to one another, churches have been planted, bodies have been healed, broken minds have been set free, innovative business ideas have been inspired, and thousands around the world have been empowered to live like Jesus.

Why We Pray "Come, Holy Spirit"

When we pray "Come, Holy Spirit" in a time of corporate ministry or personal prayer, it is not because we don't believe the Holy Spirit is already present and active among us. This prayer is a petitioning of God, a crying out for Him, to have His way in our gathering.

We also work to neither hype up a time of ministry, nor be afraid of how people respond in their humanity to the Spirit's activity in their lives. We distinguish between the Holy Spirit and the human response which shares in all the beauty and brokenness of our humanity. We believe that as we experience His presence through Christ by the Spirit we will be made more fully human and better reflections of the God-image that we were created to be.

Without the Holy Spirit active in our churches, and without our willingness to allow the Spirit to work in various ways in the contexts of our local churches, we believe we have nothing to offer to the world.

As one leader has said, "...The Church of God needs the power of God to fulfill the mandate of God in the world."

A PERSONAL REFLECTION
Di Leman

"Simply put, I love the Holy Spirit! I am grateful every day for His empowering presence living in me. I was first introduced to the Spirit in

THE VINEYARD DNA

1977, five years after becoming a disciple of Jesus.

The Spirit swept all across the U.S. during the Charismatic Renewal, touching us here in Central Illinois. Of course, He had been active in my life long before I met Him, but I barely knew a thing about Him. Being baptized in the Holy Spirit radically – and I mean radically – changed my life.

He made the Word come alive, showed me Jesus is a Healer, and gave me fresh confidence to pray. And now, over 37 years later, He continues to bring miraculous transformation in and through me. So much of my growth in the Spirit is due to my Vineyard family, who I discovered in 1982. The Vineyard showed me I could be filled again and again (not just one time), having a true river of living water flowing out of me at all times.

The Vineyard equipped me to naturally, supernaturally share the Gospel and freely ask, 'Can I pray for you right now?' putting my trust in the Holy Spirit to bring just the right gifts needed for the person I am praying for at that moment.

The Vineyard taught me to welcome the Spirit as my Teacher, my Helper, my Comforter and my Advocate, every single day of my life. And the Vineyard gave me courage to pray unashamedly for thousands of people over the years to be filled with the Spirit, speak in an unknown language, and move in His gifts.

But, more than all of the above, the Vineyard encourages me to intimately know the triune God through the Spirit. The Spirit reveals my Abba, Father, and teaches me to worship Him in spirit and in truth. The Spirit pours deep love for Jesus into my heart and makes known His grace in my life. The Spirit prays for me when I do not know how to pray, aligning my life with the Father's perfect will, causing all to work together for my good.

And, this precious, powerful Holy Spirit fills me every day with His nature and character, empowering me to reflect Jesus wherever I go, whatever I do. Jesus did not leave us as orphans but He has come to live permanently inside us. It baffles me that people still debate about and reject the Holy Spirit. I, for one, cannot live without Him. 'Come, Holy Spirit. I love you!'"

LEARNING TO RESPOND TO THE SPIRIT

Putting The Spirit At The Center

Central to the Vineyard's understanding of how we "do church" with the Holy Spirit in the lead is this one, important idea. We believe that we can *learn and grow in our capacity to discern the Spirit's activity all around us.*

To do this, we cultivate an awareness that we call "looking for what the Father is doing." When we see Jesus at work in someone's life, whether it be a neighbor whose heart is becoming soft to God during a painful divorce, or a child beginning to lead his or her peers in faith, we want to be quick to partner with the Spirit in that work in the person's life.

One early story in the Vineyard illustrates this well. John Wimber was praying for a woman after a service who had arthritis and some problems with her digestive tract. As John began to pray, he had a sense from the Lord that the woman was angry with someone.

When he asked her about it, she definitively said she was not angry with anyone. John, listening to the Holy Spirit and the impressions forming in him, asked her if she was angry with her sister.

The woman was shocked. "How did you know about that?" she asked. She went on to share the bitterness she was holding toward her sister. John prayed with her, encouraging her to forgive her sister. The woman went away and later wrote a letter to her sister.

When the letter hit the mailbox, "her pain began to subside. Within three days, all the symptoms of her illnesses had disappeared" (Wimber, *Kingdom Mercy*, p. 33-34).

Becoming Sensitive To The Spirit

As we grow in listening and looking for what the Father is doing, we can become increasingly more sensitive to the Spirit's activity. If we believe that the Father is always at work, we as Christians can learn to perceive what God is doing and to join Him in his work.

This takes practice. We have many stories in our history in which a person had a picture show up in their mind of a part of someone's body that needed healing. When the person shared it in a time of prayer ministry, a person in the room had that exact ailment and received prayer. In many cases, the recipient was healed. When people allow God to use them in others' lives, Hope enters the room.

Learning to respond to the Spirit doesn't just happen in church settings. As we cultivate a life of personal prayer, purity, and worship, our hearts are sensitized to the whispers of the Holy Spirit everywhere we go.

When we go out in public, in our neighborhoods, schools, grocery stores, and workplaces, God often has gifts He wants to give to those who don't yet know Him. This is one of the great privileges of learning to hear the Spirit's voice. We can join Him in touching someone's life in a dramatic way.

We have many stories across our international Vineyard family of the Holy Spirit speaking a very specific word of insight to a person for a non-Christian, who then shares what the Lord spoke with that person. Often, the insight is exactly applicable to the person's situation, and the individual is so touched that God would care that much, that he or she comes to faith in Jesus.

Sometimes people come to faith in Jesus when a believer, with a sense that he or she is to pray for a non-Christian's illness, asks God to bring healing. In many cases, the person is completely healed! After someone is healed, we have found that the person is very open to God's leadership in his or her life, and comes to faith in Christ.

We call these "power encounters," and often God uses our local church communities to reach people through these kinds of signs and wonders.

We Can All Welcome The Spirit

But these average people in our congregations aren't spiritual super heroes. They are just everyday Christians taking Jesus at his word. They are mothers, children, mechanics, business people, medical professionals, and more – who are learning to obey the voice of the Holy Spirit.

Jesus said He would send power from on high to equip His Church, and He was faithful to follow through. Now we, as the Body of Christ, can become people led by His Spirit in all of life. In our worship, in our prayers, we can be aware of God's presence in us and with us.

A PERSONAL REFLECTION
Mike Turrigiano

"I first became a Christian in a Pentecostal chapel service. It was loud, lively, and very expressive. Coming from a quiet Roman Catholic background, this Pentecostal style took some getting used to. Particularly strange was the way they prayed. Folks shouted, waved their hands and jumped around! I was told this was what it looked like when the Spirit showed up and did His thing.

At first, this boisterousness didn't matter to me. I was desperate for whatever contact with the Spirit I could get, and if it meant getting a little weird, so be it. And God did meet me and began changing my life. But as time went on I grew more uncomfortable with what seemed to be showy, strange, and sometimes manipulative behavior.

I loved Jesus and the people in the church, but I didn't like the package. It wasn't me. Eventually, I became gun shy and avoided the Spirit and anything that might smack of weirdness – like prophesying, praying for the sick, or casting out demons. I may have been more comfortable – but I lost something.

When I ran into John Wimber, I saw something different. John wasn't interested in wowing the crowd. There was no hype, weirdness or manipulation. When he ministered, he was relaxed, comfortable, real. I was impressed with how he remained normal while worshipping and praying. John called it being 'naturally supernatural.'

John was the same person during ministry time that he was during dinnertime. I learned that I didn't have to put on some spiritual persona, change the tone of my voice when I prayed, or get frenzied in order for the Spirit to move.

And the most significant and liberating discovery was that I could just be myself and God would still show up! I could respond to the promptings of the Spirit in my own, authentic way. That was huge! My response to this freedom was, 'I can do that! I want to do that!' I was off and running, 'doing the stuff' of the Kingdom, and I haven't stopped since.

Being naturally supernaturally has become a Vineyard distinctive. It's fundamental to who we are for several reasons:

* *It means everyone gets to play. You can be uniquely yourself, and God can still use you.*

* *It relieves the pressure to perform. You can act normal, and God will still show up.*

* *It opens up ministry opportunities out in the marketplace of life, not just inside the church.*

* *Outsiders don't feel intimidated or put off by prayer because there's no weirdness, hype or manipulation. Receptivity to God increases dramatically.*

* *And finally, being naturally supernatural paves the way for people to actually experience God's loving and healing presence in a way that feels neither threatening nor embarrassing.*

THE VINEYARD DNA

In our secular world, where often a person's only reference for the supernatural is Hollywood fantasy and reality TV weirdness, the comfort of God's Spirit being exhibited in naturally supernatural ways is for many the start of a faith journey of their own."

BECOMING PEOPLE OF THE SPIRIT

The Presence Of God Points Us Forward

As was said at the beginning, we in the Vineyard are a "people of the presence of God." We see our lives as Christians being shaped by the Holy Spirit guiding us in life and ministry. The presence and activity of the Spirit is always pointing us toward the day when disease will be gone, lives will be restored, and God's purposes for the world will be fulfilled.

When we build our lives on the Spirit's work in and through us, we are building our lives on God's future Kingdom.

Because of this reality, intractable issues in individual lives, such as disease or mental oppression, we see as opportunities to partner with the Holy Spirit in Kingdom ministry. For social issues such as poverty, injustice, and sex trafficking, we address these with confidence knowing that the Holy Spirit empowers us to work with Him in humanizing and dignifying our fellow human beings.

As Christians, we value the Word of God, the Bible, as our guide in character, life, and practice. We also value the Spirit of God, the third Person of the Trinity, in our ministry and Kingdom activity.

As an old adage says, "The Word without the Spirit – we *dry* up.

The Spirit without the Word – we *blow* up. The Word and the Spirit together – we *grow* up." We are committed to being a people who are "empowered Evangelicals," embracing the rich gifts of the Scriptures and embracing the tension that comes with living as Spirit-led people.

From the beginning, Vineyard pastors and leaders have sought to hold in tension the biblical doctrines of the Christian faith with an ardent pursuit of the present day work of the Spirit of God. Maintaining that balance is never easy in the midst of rapid growth and renewal.

We have chosen not to seek the *power* of God in what we do, but rather to seek the *presence* of God in all we do. In God's presence is the power to do what He invites us to do.

With our values at center, we are seeking to take our place in the Body of Christ, serving alongside those who truly desire to experience the Holy Spirit actively working in and through their everyday lives.

A PERSONAL REFLECTION
Brenda Gatlin

"My journey with the Holy Spirit began a little over 26 years ago when I discovered that God was passionate about me experiencing a personal, meaningful, authentic, and genuine relationship with Him. In my first Vineyard church, I began to hear that God wanted me to experience His presence through a friendship with the Holy Spirit. Today, I relate to Him daily and nurture a friendship with Him. Here are my favorite things about having the Holy Spirit in my life:

THE VINEYARD DNA

1. He is the one who makes it possible for me to experience and relate to God the Father.

Romans 5:5 says, '...God has poured out his love into our hearts by the Holy Spirit, whom he has given us.' Without the Spirit, we find our relationship with God becomes dry, distant, cold, and a religious ritual. The Spirit is the experienced reality of God and He makes it possible for my relationship with God to come alive. The Spirit helps us experience all the benefits of being God's children. He makes the Father become my Abba Father. Without the Holy Spirit, we would not experience God's presence. Psalm 51:11 sums it up: 'Cast me not away from your presence, and take not your Holy Spirit from me.'

2. He is the one who makes it possible to be transformed and changed from the inside out.

He's the one who begins to change me and eventually makes me start to look and sound like Jesus. Galatians 6:7-8 says, 'Don't be misled – you cannot mock the justice of God. You will always harvest what you plant. Those who live only to satisfy their own sinful nature will harvest decay and death from that sinful nature. But those who live to please the Spirit will harvest everlasting life from the Spirit. He's the one who deposits supernatural healing and help from God in me and brings wholeness and freedom to me. That results in my life beginning to show evidence of the fruits of the Spirit: love, joy, peace, and patience (Gal. 5:22-23). He's the one who begins to flow through me so that Jesus Christ, instead of my flesh, is reflected in my life.

3. He is the one who makes it possible to receive spiritual gifts and do things that Jesus did.

He releases the gifts in me, nurtures the gifts in me, and breathes on the gifts in me. If there is not a release of spiritual gifts, then I have no real authentic expression of God's heart and am lacking in Kingdom fruit. The Spirit allows me to be the hands and feet of Jesus to the people that Jesus wants to touch through me. As I learn to receive His Spirit, my gifts are nurtured and I can become who God meant for me to be. I can express God's heart to others freely giving what He's given me.

4. He is absolutely all-inclusive, available, and accessible to anyone who acknowledges their need for Him.

To experience His presence all we have to do is acknowledge our need for Him and turn towards Him (this often includes repenting and renouncing pride). A simple and humble prayer of 'Holy Spirit come, I welcome you here now' ushers us immediately into God's presence. This is what Jesus meant when He said, 'The Kingdom of God is at hand.' Humbly walking with our God means we are learning to be intimate and dependent on His Spirit by turning toward Him, and dwelling in His presence.

5. The Holy Spirit is my friend and in His presence, there is peace.

Peace is a state of tranquility, freedom from disturbance, a state of security, and freedom from oppressive thoughts or emotions. Our spirits are starved for the gift of peace. It's restful, and there is no other place to find true peace, outside of the presence of the Holy Spirit. Romans 8:6 says, 'For to set the mind on the flesh is death, but to set the mind on the Spirit is life and peace.'"

THE VINEYARD DNA

A PERSONAL REFLECTION
Caleb Maskell

"'It is better for you that I go away' (John 16:7).

What do you think it must have been like for Jesus' disciples to hear him say these words? For years, they had given up their whole lives to follow him, to learn from him, to watch him work. Jesus was the most compelling, ingenious, compassionate, free person they had ever known. He was what they wanted – there was no one else like him. 'Where else can we go, Lord?' said the apostle Peter, 'You have the words of life.'

And yet now, Jesus said he was leaving them. How could that possibly be 'better'?

Jesus tried to explain: 'If I go, God the Father will send you a Helper in my place, the Holy Spirit. He will come to live inside each of you, giving you peace, creative power and discernment about what the Father wants to do. He will teach you things you don't know yet, and help you to do greater things than I have done. But for the Holy Spirit to come, I have to go' (from John 16:7-15).

Hmm. Who knows what the disciples were thinking? I'd bet they weren't peaceful, happy thoughts, especially as things quickly went from bad to worse. You know the story: Jesus was arrested, tried, and crucified. The disciples were scattered, terrified.

Then, it quickly got really weird. Jesus came back to life, and came to find them – just as they were on the brink of giving up on him. He ate with them, fished with them, let them touch his wounds to prove that he was really alive, forgave them for abandoning him. Mind-blowing stuff.

After a few days together, he left them again, returning to his Father in heaven. But just before he did, he reminded them of the plan: Stay in Jerusalem and wait for the Holy Spirit. So they obeyed. They waited. They prayed by faith – 'Come, Holy Spirit.' Some among them were afraid. Some were confused. Some were hopeful. Some doubted. Some were exhausted. All believed somewhat, but some didn't know what to believe. They were a ragtag bunch, knocked sideways by history; hardly a perfect team of spiritual giants.

But what they did do was show up, obedient, with their battered, uneven faith, to wait for what Jesus had promised. Bringing whatever they had – coming just as they were. And, the Holy Spirit came, the Church was born, and giants they became. (If you want to know the rest, read the book of Acts.)

I love that 'Come, Holy Spirit' is not a prayer by which strong people give orders to God, calling him to act in endorsement of their ministry or mission. It is the opposite, actually. It comes to us as the cry of a desperate Church, undone by the love and power of Jesus and eager to serve him as the King. Without the Holy Spirit, they were utterly bereft. But with the Holy Spirit, they changed the world forever.

Come, Holy Spirit."

CHAPTER 5
REMEMBER THE POOR

Over the decades of the Vineyard's existence, the poor have featured prominently in the way we think about God's mission on the earth. Why? And why have the poor, vulnerable, and marginalized in society become so central to the way Vineyard communities do life and allocate resources?

A Biblical View Of The Poor

Who are the poor? Today, we often see poverty through the lens of economics or personal financial weakness. In the New Testament, however, the poor are generally seen as those who are powerless in society, and who therefore lack the basic necessities they need to sustain their lives.

Without resources, and without a voice, they lack not only power, but also social respect and material goods. Because of the daily stresses of survival, relationships often break down. Poverty is a disease of society, and the remedies for all our social ills are found in the life and teaching of Jesus.

In the Scriptures, it seems that God has a special place in His heart for the poor. Poverty is mentioned, directly or indirectly, more than 2000 times in the Bible. Reminding us of the Church's call to care for the marginalized and impoverished among us, Jesus said words that pierce us to this day:

"...'Truly I tell you, whatever you did for one of the least of these brothers and sisters of mine, you did for me'" (Matt. 25:40).

The Vineyard family of churches leans toward the poor, the outcast, and the outsider with the compassion of Jesus. From the beginning of our movement, Vineyard churches have worked to actively serve the poor in the most practical ways possible – in our towns, cities, and spheres of influence. John Wimber, the founder of the Vineyard, was personally committed to calling us to a radically compassionate life in the way of Jesus.

In the Vineyard, we believe that faithfulness to Jesus means that we are faithful to remember the poor, serve the poor, build community among the poor – and love the poor compelled by the love of God.

WHAT JESUS SAID ABOUT THE POOR

Jesus Spends Time With The Poor
In the Gospels, we see Jesus spending a considerable amount of time among the poor, serving them, encouraging them, and even standing

up for them. He was carrying on the deep, rich, Jewish, biblical tradition of providing for those in need.

These words from the book of Deuteronomy reveal God's tenderness toward the socially vulnerable:

"He defends the cause of the fatherless and the widow, and loves the alien, giving him food and clothing" (Deut. 10:18).

"If there is a poor man among your brothers in any of the towns of the land that the Lord your God is giving you, do not be hardhearted or tightfisted toward your poor brother. Rather be openhanded and freely lend him whatever he needs" (Deut. 15:7-8).

"There will always be poor people in the land. Therefore I command you to be openhanded toward your brothers and toward the poor and needy in your land" (Deut. 15:11).

"Is not this the kind of fasting I have chosen: to loose the chains of injustice and untie the cords of the yoke, to set the oppressed free and break every yoke? Is it not to share your food with the hungry and to provide the poor wanderer with shelter – when you see the naked, to clothe them, and not to turn away from your own flesh and blood?" (Is. 58:6-7).

The Poor In The Gospels
From these roots, Jesus calls the early Church to commit to seek out the poor and dignify them with their care:

"Looking at his disciples he said: 'Blessed are you who are poor, for yours is the Kingdom of God'" (Luke 6:20).

"The Spirit of the Lord is on me, because he has anointed me to preach good news to the poor. He has sent me to proclaim freedom for the prisoners and recovery of sight for the blind, to release the oppressed" (Luke 4:18).

"...But when you give a banquet, invite the poor, the crippled, the lame, the blind, and you will be blessed. Although they cannot repay you, you will be repaid at the resurrection of the righteous" (Luke 14:13-14).

The Poor In The New Testament

Following Jesus' example, the apostles and the early Church embody Jesus' love for the poor:

"All they asked was that we should continue to remember the poor, the very thing I had been eager to do all along" (Gal. 2:10).

"Share with God's people who are in need. Practice hospitality" (Rom. 12:13).

"Listen, my dear brothers: Has not God chosen those who are poor in the eyes of the world to be rich in faith and to inherit the Kingdom he promised those who love him?" (James 2:5).

"Religion that God our Father accepts as pure and faultless is this: to look after orphans and widows in their distress and to keep oneself from being polluted by the world" (James 1:27).

A Movement That Cares For The Poor

After Jesus' resurrection, in the earliest years of the Church, the Roman government struggled to care for the masses of widows and orphans overrunning their society. Motivated by Jesus' model, and realizing that the poor were to be welcomed as Jesus Himself, the early Christians addressed the issues of social struggle surrounding orphans and widows.

Some scholars suggest this may have been the primary reason the Church grew like wildfire in its first century of life.

Since those early days, the Church has been marked by our care for the least, the last, and the lost. When the marginalized and forgotten of any society are brought into the focus of a loving community that worships Christ, powerful things begin to happen.

Jesus has called us to care for the poor – both for their sake and our own.

A PERSONAL REFLECTION
Lance & Cheryl Pittluck

"There can be little argument that the goal of the Christian life is to be more like Jesus, to act and think, to respond, and speak like Jesus. And therefore, we must also aim for the priorities of Jesus.

'The Spirit of the Lord is on me, because he has anointed me to preach good news to the poor. He has sent me to proclaim freedom for the prisoners and recovery of sight for the blind, to release the oppressed' (Luke 4:18).

We preach, and we preach good news, and we preach good news to the poor, I hope. But reaching out to the poor doesn't necessarily come naturally. Unless 'the poor' are your family, friends and immediate community, it's easy to not give them much thought. They often go unheard, not having a voice in society. They may not shop where we shop, hang out in the places where we socialize, or even attend our churches. And yet, they are to be a primary concern to us, as they are to God.

'For he will deliver the needy who cry out, the afflicted who have no one to help. He will take pity on the weak and the needy and save the needy from death. He will rescue them from oppression and violence, for precious is their blood in his sight' (Ps. 72:12-14).

The answer seems obvious that we are to make a concerted effort to carry out God's commands to love, serve and minister to the poor. Taking our faith out into the streets may mean searching for the streets that are hidden from our daily lives. It requires a missionary mentality... the kind of thinking and planning that goes into ministry to another culture different from our own.

Because that is what poverty is, a culture. The poor live by different rules, having learned to survive with less than they need – less money and material possessions, but also less education, tools, opportunities, and options. And before we can really serve them, we have to learn from them what it means to be poor, and who they are.

'Is not this the kind of fasting I have chosen: to loose the chains of injustice and untie the cords of the yoke, to set the oppressed free and break every yoke?' (Is. 58:6). How do I minister to you? I get to know you, spend time with you, listen, ask questions and even share from my own life. And I have to show you that I care and can be trusted. This takes time, persistence, consistency and commitment.

THE VINEYARD DNA

How do we minister to the poor? We meet them, befriend them, listen to and learn from them, love and serve them, and invite them into our family to share what we have – the hope and promise and freedom that comes from living in the light and love of God.

'For the Lord is the Spirit, and wherever the Spirit of the Lord is, there is freedom' (2 Cor. 3:17)."

WHAT THE POOR MEAN TO US

Giving What We Have Been Given

We lean toward the lost, the poor, the outcast, and the outsider with the compassion of Jesus as sinners whose only standing before God is utterly dependent on the mercy of God. This mercy can only be truly received inasmuch as we are willing to give it away.

In other words, we as a church movement *lean toward* those who are suffering and are weak in society. We do so not because we believe we are better than them, or because we believe we can fix them. We lean toward the poor, the outcast, and the outsider because we ourselves have experienced the kindness and mercy of God.

God did not look at each one of us and decide to show us mercy based on whether or not we had gotten ourselves into a mess, or even because we were blameless and someone else had done something to us. He simply looked on us with love, then acted in compassion to rescue us from the kingdom of darkness.

Grateful people, who know the joy of their salvation, tend to be more careful when it comes to judging others. In the Vineyard we seek to be a thankful group of people, so that when we see someone in need our hearts are ready to respond with care rather than judgment. As Jesus said, "He who is forgiven much, loves much" (Luke 7:47). Through our spiritual practices as churches, we want to become people who love much.

The Poor Are Jesus To Us

What do the poor mean to us? In the profound moment when Jesus said, "...Whatever you did for one of the least of these brothers and sisters of mine, you did for me" (Matt. 25:40), He was teaching us how to see the poor. We see the poor not primarily as the underprivileged or the needy, but rather as Jesus. Like Mother Theresa, who regularly cared for the poor in Calcutta, India, Vineyard churches generate ministries around the globe that see the poor as Jesus – and are serving them with great dignity.

A story about John Wimber illustrates this tenderness toward the poor. John was known for keeping a bag of basic groceries in the trunk of his car and looking for someone to whom he could give them. He even once said,

"Many Christians and Christian leaders have been neutralized by the love of money and materialism. The homage paid to affluence becomes a burden that saps our energy as well as our love for God and other people. Through repentance and the cleansing of forgiveness, we can rid ourselves of this burden and begin to let God transform our value system. Like Jesus and Paul, we can learn to be content with what we have, living modestly in order that we may give liberally to the work of the Kingdom and to meet the needs of others."

It is in this spirit that we seek to operate as churches. Because the poor mean much to Jesus, we must seek out those who are the most in need around us. With the resources in our hands, we desire to invest in Good News being shared with the poor – both spiritually and materially.

Lifting People From Poverty And Injustice

Of course, this will look differently in different places. Poverty means many different things in different parts of the world. Vineyard churches exist in these places, and it is part of our genetic code to join Jesus in His mission to "seek and save the lost" (Luke 19:10).

For this reason you will find Vineyard communities caring for the poor as though caring for themselves, eagerly sharing their resources to help lift people from poverty and injustice.

A PERSONAL REFLECTION
Brian & Thora Anderson

"John Wimber once said, 'If you're not going to care for the poor, then don't use the Vineyard name.' We have taken that statement seriously since early on in our church and have tried to care for the poor in some way.

Ministry to the poor in a church almost always starts small. It certainly did with us. We began giving a little bit of food away on Saturdays out of a closet that we had in one of our first rented buildings. Over time, that closet ended up growing into a larger space, and then a larger space, and then a larger space.

When we felt God was wanting us to build the auditorium we are in now, we felt like God wanted us to build an entire building that was used to minister to the poor. And, we felt God told us to make sure we built that first, before we built the new auditorium or added more children's ministry space. So, that's what we did.

Since that time, our ministry to the poor has evolved into a ministry that reaches thousands of families each year, in all kinds of different ways. We have a food and clothing bank that is open six days a week. We have a free medical clinic open every Saturday afternoon. We do multiple large ministry outreaches to our community including our annual Thanksgiving Outreach. (Last year we gave out over 1,200 complete turkey dinners, which fed 5-6,000 people.)

We also partner with our city to paint houses for the elderly, and we hand out hundreds of backpacks and school supplies in our annual Back to School Outreach, along with free ESL classes, tax assistance, resume writing, and job placement. In today's economic landscape it is crucial that churches show the love of Jesus in tangible ways to their surrounding communities!

Caring for the poor is in the genetic make-up of the Vineyard. Our hope is that all Vineyard churches take that seriously, care for the poor, and see what amazing ways God multiplies their efforts!"

HOW CAN WE SERVE THE POOR?

Getting Involved With The Poor

There is so much injustice in our world today, we can feel paralyzed by the sheer scope of the need. Yet if we ignore injustice, and turn our backs on the powerless and the poor, the Scripture tells us that something very sad happens. God hears our worship as "noise" until we *"...Let justice roll on like a river; righteousness like a never-failing stream"* (Amos 5:34).

But how can you and I get involved? Amid the thousands of images of suffering we see on our streets, televisions, phones, and computer screens, how do we choose where we will invest our lives?

Here, the words of Jesus can move us forward: "Give and it will be given to you" (Luke 6:38). In other words, if we just start giving – giving time, resources, and energy to those in need – God will both guide us and give us what we need to do His will.

Across the Vineyard Movement, there are literally hundreds of ways to be involved in caring for those in need. We have ministries that address the sex trafficking industry, poor health and sanitation issues, economic injustice, racial injustice, and issues of spiritual poverty. Vineyard communities are committed to innovating new expressions of ministry for the world's most vulnerable to get the resources they need.

Faith Is Spelled R-I-S-K

Many years ago, Carol Wimber used the language of the "haves" and the "have nots" when speaking about the Vineyard's call to serve the poor. One day, we are the "haves," with food on our table, peace in our home, and provision for our education.

On another day, we might be the "have nots," in need of someone to share their resources and influence to help us change the circumstance we are in. The "have nots" need the" haves" for their supply, but the "haves" need the "have nots" to give meaning to the gifts that God has place in their hands.

In your community, either through your local Vineyard church or through a relief organization, there are opportunities to get beyond your comfort zone and to get involved.

For many years, Vineyard churches have spelled faith: R-I-S-K. Sometimes we must jump off the diving board before we know if there is water in the pool! Finding God in the midst of a new adventure means diving in and trusting that God will help you as you do.

Our Vineyard history is rich with literally thousands of stories of people who encountered Jesus and His Kingdom through someone reaching out to them with care. In Vineyards around the world, we often match people's life experience with a need. For example, if you are a young woman then perhaps ministering to young women rescued from the sex trafficking industry is a next step for you. If you have known the difficulty of joblessness, it is possible that a great start for you would be to work with the homeless and jobless of your city.

Sharing some of our experiences with others in need can break down invisible barriers, creating supportive relationships. Often, God uses our stories to open the heart of another to Jesus – giving an opportunity for the Holy Spirit to provide for them in ways no one else can.

Joining The Father Among The Poor

Our desire as a movement is not to ask God to bless what we are doing in our churches, but rather to get involved in what God is already doing. We see God's heart for the poor, and we see Him moving among the weak to bring deliverance and healing through His people.

In fact, many of our churches around the world are building their faith communities among the poor, integrating with those in need as neighbors, friends, and brothers and sisters in Christ. Long-term care, job placement, and enrichment paths are set in motion, and those broken by poverty or abuse often rise to become healthy, hopeful, and healing followers of Christ.

Get involved caring for the poor in your local context, with a humble heart to serve. You'll be amazed at what changes in you as you follow Jesus among the poor.

A PERSONAL REFLECTION
David Ruis

"I have a distinct memory of sitting in my study one day as I was pulling together thoughts and materials related to stepping out on yet another church planting adventure. I was quite excited, feeling that rush of risking faith that these types of pioneering ventures demand, ready to pull together my demographics, cultural analyses and various and sundry cool ideas that I was envisioning for this new emerging community.

In the midst of the swirl of documents, scribbles, ear-tagged books, notes and the latest DVDs –on everything from relevant communication trends to systems and community development – was my Bible. Open.

Staring up at me were the words given to Paul as he was launching on his first foray into church planting and mission. Peter, James and John, considered to be the pillars of the early Church in every regard, agreed that it was time for Paul to step out. To risk. To put his hand to the call on his life to participate in the expanding Kingdom of heaven through missional endeavors out into the Gentile world far out of the reach of Jerusalem and Samaria.

Their words of instruction to Paul were there on the page burning not just into my eyes, but into my heart as well.

As Paul would step out he would become the first intentional missionary and church planter in the history of the Church. The Gospel had spread to many places of the world through persecution and the dispersion of believers for various reasons. But this was a first. This was important. The key elements of the Gospel of the Kingdom must be proclaimed and modeled.

Pretty big stuff.

The thing Peter, James and John said to Paul was not just gripping my heart, but shifting my thinking. In fact, the more I pondered what I was reading, I began to get somewhat angry as I looked up in my study to see, as Wimber would say, 'words, words, words, words' – so much instruction; teaching; training information about faith; life and the church. I couldn't remember anyone in the midst of all these 'words' telling me what Paul was told.

I was ticked. Why had I never heard this before?

'All they asked was that we should continue to remember the poor, the very thing that I was eager to do all along' (Paul the Apostle, Gal. 2:10).

THE VINEYARD DNA

That's all they asked. Full stop. At the one-year evaluation as to how things at your church are going, there is only one question on the exam. At the two-year point, just one question still. At the 10-year mark, there is just one requirement that cannot be lost in the midst of all the challenges and hurdles of living out faith and building community:

Did you remember the poor?

The more I walk this journey in my own life and in the midst of the community of faith I realize that this one simple request is more and more central than I ever dreamed to the understanding of the Gospel, the call to follow Christ, and the mission of the Church.

Remember the poor. Don't forget the poor."

BECOMING A COMPASSIONATE PEOPLE

Suffering With Others

Compassion is a word we often use in the Vineyard to sum up the kind of Christians we want to become. Jesus "had compassion" on the harassed and helpless (Matt. 9:36), and this moves us to want to have compassion in all that we do as churches.

Compassion literally means "to suffer with." When we learn to suffer with those in physical distress, or economic pain, over time we begin to carry God's heart for the poor. Compassion is learned by doing the work of the Kingdom – the work of serving the poor.

This takes moving beyond mere sympathy for the poor. Compassion is a motivation of the heart that gets our hands dirty, and causes us to live in a way that is contrary to a world turning its applause toward anyone with celebrity status, wealth, or reputation.

Hear these words from the prophet Isaiah, that reveal a promise from God when we act compassionately in the world He loves:

"Is not this the kind of fasting I have chosen: to loose the chains of injustice and untie the cords of the yoke, to set the oppressed free and break every yoke? Is it not to share your food with the hungry and to provide the poor wanderer with shelter — when you see the naked, to clothe them, and not to turn away from your own flesh and blood?

Then your light will break forth like the dawn, and your healing will quickly appear; then your righteousness will go before you, and the glory of the Lord will be your rear guard. Then you will call, and the Lord will answer; you will cry for help, and he will say: Here am I" (Is. 58:6-9).

We can practice radical hospitality, radical welcome to those in need, just as the early Church did. We can seek out those who are marginalized by society (even by churches) and treat them with dignity and honor.

We can see the lost, the poor, the outcast, and the outsider through the loving eyes of Jesus. In fact, we can even see the poor as Jesus Himself (Matt. 25:40).

When we remember the poor, when we serve the poor – we are serving Christ.

CHAPTER 6
WHAT IS WORSHIP?

When people are talking about the distinctive qualities of the Vineyard family of churches, one word may rise above the rest in the conversation – *worship*.

The Vineyard Movement has been known for its expressions of intimate, powerful, and values-rich worship music across the global Church for decades. Worship is central to all we do in the Vineyard.

A Vineyard Worship Experience
If you have ever attended a worship gathering in a local Vineyard church setting, you may have noticed a few things during your experience.

As the musical part of the worship service began, you may have sensed anticipation in the congregation, like they were looking forward to what was about to happen. It's possible the worship leader communicated a sense of closeness and familiarity with God in his or her prayers, and that the leader was eager for the congregation to experience God in worship.

As those gathered began to sing, you may also have observed the uninhibited expressions of love freely being offered by the worshippers, and the music taking on almost a supportive place. As the songs played on, you may have thought that the people in the room seemed to be aware of God being present with them, that worship was *interactive*.

You may have noted those gathered were having an encounter with God as they sang songs about loving Jesus. Words of adoration, thanksgiving, and confession may have been sung or spoken, in simple or poetic ways. You may have seen people all around you with hands raised, singing passionately, or on their knees in devotion.

As the leader started and finished each song, you might have observed an absence of hype or stirring up of emotion from the crowd. Maybe you sang for 20, 30, or even 45 minutes, moving in and out of songs with fluidity, as if they were prayers rather than just musical presentations.

On the lyric screen, it's possible you noticed that many of the songs being sung were published by Vineyard Worship or a group with Vineyard in the name.

Phrases like "the Kingdom of God," "I love you," and "Holy Spirit, come" may have been in the lyrics. After the message, as a time of prayer for individuals began, the band may have begun to play, accompanying a time of compassionate ministry.

If any part of what you just read is true of your experience, then you've probably already begun to taste the heart of what it means to us – as a Vineyard family – to worship.

In the following pages, we'll look briefly at who we worship, why we worship, and how we worship – all from a Vineyard perspective. Then, we'll weave all those ideas together as we look at worship through the unique values of the Vineyard Movement.

By the time you are finished, may you find your heart filled with a desire to express your love to God as He has expressed His love to you. The heart is where worship always begins.

WHO DO WE WORSHIP?

Early Encounters With God

The Vineyard Movement has been said to be among the most significant early influencers of the contemporary worship movements of today. Over the last 30-40 years, experiencing God in gathered worship has been a hallmark of the Vineyard Movement. This comes directly from our roots.

When the Vineyard Movement was in its earliest years, John and Carol Wimber (John is regarded as the founding leader of the Vineyard) were meeting with a small gathering of worn-out leaders. They were all moved to deep repentance before God. As they spent time together worshipping and singing songs to God (rather than just about God), they experienced God's presence in deeply profound and personal ways. It is here that Vineyard worship was born.

Songs of intimate worship became a primary language of prayer for these broken people in those early days, and that love for experiencing God through worship music is now part of the genetic code of the Vineyard.

A Life-Giving Interchange

In those early gatherings, singing to God in worship was personal, and worship had as much (or more) to do with the "broken and contrite heart" (Ps. 51:17) of the person worshipping as it did with any melody being sung. Though John was a professional musician and known for his expertise as a producer, his understanding of worship always had to do first with God's love, and our response to it. Simple worship songs seemed to help that life-giving interchange happen.

For that reason, Vineyard worship expressions have always been primarily musical in nature, and intimate in posture. In the Vineyard, the music facilitates the real point of why we've gathered – to meet face to face with the God of the Scriptures.

Who We Worship

When we worship, we make Christ the central focus of our affection. We sense God's presence with us, the Spirit of God touching us, and communicating to us the Father's love. The Bible shows us the nature of the glorious God we worship:

We worship God as Creator (Gen. 1:1) – the Father, maker and sustainer of all life, who began all things, and will bring history to its consummation.

THE VINEYARD DNA

We worship God as King (Ps. 103:19) – the Lord and Sovereign over the cosmos, the benevolent leader of His Kingdom, and the One extending His rule through people who love Him and obey His word.

We worship God as Trinity (Deut. 6:4) – One God expressing Himself in three Persons, dwelling in perfect harmony within the Godhead – Father, Son, and Holy Spirit.

We worship God as Savior (Matt. 1:21) – the rescuing God who by Jesus' life, death on a cross, and resurrection conquers sin and death, making us new creations in Christ.

All of these attributes of God inform our worship, from the way we prepare our hearts for the activity of worship, to the songs we write and choose for our set lists.

Worship is an end in itself – it is our opportunity to surrender ourselves again and again to our amazing God.

To use an analogy from the world of grammar, God is the *Subject* of worship – the One who initiates the worship interaction and acts in love (the verb) toward us, the *Objects* of His affection. We then respond in love, telling God how grateful we are to Him for all He has done, and is doing, in our lives.

As the adage says, we become like who or what we worship.

Through worship, we want to become like Jesus.

WHAT IS WORSHIP? QUOTES

"...Worship, the act of freely giving love to God, forms and informs every activity of the Christian's life. Many people who visit Vineyard Christian Fellowships remark on the depth and richness of our worship. This has not come about by chance: we have a well-thought-out philosophy that guides why and how we worship God...."
- JOHN WIMBER

"...After we started to meet in our home gathering, I noticed times during the meeting – usually when we sang – in which I experienced God deeply. We sang many songs, but mostly songs about worship or testimonies from one Christian to another. But occasionally we sang a song personally and intimately to Jesus, with lyrics like 'Jesus I love you.' Those types of songs both stirred and fed the hunger for God within me...."
- CAROL WIMBER

"...Songs are an indicator for us in the Vineyard. The songs coming forth from our churches show what God's doing among us as a people. I always watch and listen to the songs to make sure the fire never goes out on the altar. If there's fire on the songs, it's always a good sign to me."
- CAROL WIMBER

"For the Vineyard family of churches, experiencing God in the midst of personal or corporate worship has always been one of our core values. We are, at our very foundation, a people who find their greatest identity, strength, and joy in the presence of God ."
- PHIL STROUT

"We can never pin worship into a service. Just when you think you have God cornered, the Living One has gone somewhere else. So you run after

Him, and you find Him in a place you never expected, or you see His face in the poor. Our journey is one of life, and our worship is a living sacrifice before a living God. That is a life of simple devotion to Christ."
- DAVID RUIS

"One thing I ask from the Lord, this only do I seek: that I may dwell in the house of the Lord all the days of my life, to gaze on the beauty of the Lord and to seek Him in His temple."
- PSALM 27:4

WHY DO WE WORSHIP?

We Are The Pursued
If you ask anyone who is attending church on a Sunday morning, "Why do we worship?" you'll probably get a variety of answers.

In the Vineyard Movement, we believe the answer to this question is found in one short passage in 1 John 4:19. Though it is translated in a few different ways, the NKJV says this:

> *"We love Him, because He first loved us."*

In those eight words we find not only the answer to why we worship, but also what it means to be God's child.

We express our love to God in worship not because we started this love relationship – but because God did! From Genesis to Revelation, God reveals Himself to be the Pursuer of your heart and mine. It is He who first loved us and pursued us, and it is we who are the objects of His undying affection.

Worship is a simple response to God's unconditional love. We can complicate worship in a thousand ways, but we will always come back to this truth.

When we truly understand this reality, that God is the One who initiates the loving communion that is worship, it changes us. Rather than trying to gain God's approval by fulfilling religious obligations and doing the *right* things in worship, we can rest in knowing that God loves us before we even do one thing! Worship creates an environment in which we can let go of our striving, and fall into the loving arms of the Father.

Like a child being hugged by a parent, we hear the words, "I love you, not because of what you do, but because of who you are!" When the Samaritan woman asks Jesus to tell her exactly how to worship in a way that would please God (John 4:19-24), Jesus responds by telling her what kind of person God is seeking as a worshipper.

Like this woman, many today think about worship in relation to the externals – the musical styles and religious habits that we think please or displease God. But God is always looking at the heart, as it is in the heart that worship begins and ends.

When we are responding to God's love, we are putting God in His rightful place as the Subject of the worship story. We then, as God reveals His love to us by His Spirit, respond to Him with love!

This cycle goes on forever.

THE VINEYARD DNA

Ways We Express Our Love

For this reason, worship in the Vineyard is always interactive, as it has to do with both God and the people gathered. It is not personality-driven, by a superstar who takes up all the attention in the room. Rather, our worship leaders seek to cultivate humility and transparency even as they seek to lead effectively and with quality in the music.

This is why, in a Vineyard worship setting, you will see people actively demonstrating their love for God by lifting their hands (like we're receiving a gift), singing passionately (like someone expressing one's love to another), or kneeling in thanks (like a person bowing to honor a King). God is our focus in worship.

These expressions above, and more, are ways we can biblically respond to God's love. As the Psalmist said, "Lift up your hands in the sanctuary and bless the Lord" (Ps. 134:2); and "Shout to the Lord..." (Ps. 98:4-6). Musical instruments and more are involved in worship as they are all tools that can help us respond to God's love.

Vineyard Songs Around The World

As an overflow of our response to God's love, the worship music of the Vineyard has circled the globe for four decades. Born in intimate communion with God in our local churches, songs like *Come, Now Is The Time To Worship*, *Hungry*, *Breathe*, *Dwell*, and *Holy And Anointed One* (and thousands of others) have given the Body of Christ songs that say what we need to say to God.

Today, new Vineyard songs continue to pour out from our churches around the world.

THE POWER OF A NEW SONG

New Songs Come From God

According to Psalm 40:3, *God* is the One who gives new songs to every generation of the Body of Christ.

"He put a new song in my mouth, a hymn of praise to our God" (Psalm 40:3).

Songs can be very powerful, in that they are memorable, repeatable, encouraging, and contain biblical and theological ideas that sustain and guide us. The following are lyric excerpts from a variety of Vineyard songs.

If you know the song from which the lyric comes, begin to sing it, and let the Holy Spirit meet you as you draw near to God through the simplicity of a melody carrying the words. Make the song your prayer as you sing.

*What joy is found // In communion with
You // Bowing in reverence*

*There is no one like You // Risen Son of
God // Holy is Your name*

*Exalt the Lord, our God // And worship at
His feet*

*You'll see me through // You're the rock
that will not be moved*

*Come, now is the time to worship // Come,
now is the time to give your heart*

*Hungry, I come to You // For I know you
satisfy*

Lead on // Lead on

*You are great and wonderful // Yes, You
are // Yes, You are*

*Open up my eyes // Let me see Your glory
// See Your glory*

*Your love is deep, Your love is wide // And
it covers us //*

*Your love is amazing // Steady and
unchanging // Your love is a mountain //
Firm beneath my feet*

*We sing // Come, Lord Jesus, come //
Come, Lord Jesus, come*

*And I surrender // All to You, all to You //
And I surrender // All to You, all to You*

*This is the air I breathe // Your holy
presence, living in me*

*Draw me close to You // Never let me go
// I lay it all down again // To hear You say
that I'm Your friend*

*Jesus, Jesus // Holy and anointed One //
Jesus*

*Faithful One // So unchanging // Ageless
One // You're my rock of peace*

*I love // I love // I love Your presence // I
love // I love // I love Your presence*

*That heals and sets me free // Pour it out
// Pour it out*

*Move us, lead us // Send us, release us //
To the broken, to the hungry*

*I want to know You // I want to hear Your
voice // I want to know You more*

Isn't He // Beautiful // Beautiful // Isn't He

HOW DO WE WORSHIP

A Life Surrendered To God

One of the most quoted passages in the Bible, related to worship, is Romans 12:1. It says:

THE VINEYARD DNA

"Therefore, I urge you, brothers and sisters, in view of God's mercy, to offer your bodies as a living sacrifice, holy and pleasing to God – this is your true and proper worship."

If there was one thing that Paul (the writer of Romans) and the people of his time understood, it was that sacrifices are *dead*. In other words, when he talks about our lives being "living sacrifices" of worship, he is literally saying, "As dead as a dead sacrifice is, that is how living your life offering to God is to be – a complete and a done deal!"

This passage is telling us, through a metaphor, that the worship God seeks involves our entire lives, offered as a response to His great love. From the way we speak to our spouses, to the way we handle our money, love our neighbors, and work at our jobs, worship is an all-encompassing act. An old Latin phrase, *coram Deo*, sums up this kind of life. It means to "live before the face of God," or to "live in the presence of God."

When we gather to worship in a Vineyard context, we see it as a time of encounter, of refreshing, of empowering in the presence of God. That encounter touches us in the deepest places of our hearts, where God's love can begin to change us from the inside out.

We find courage to live, and strength to face our greatest challenges. Because we believe that everything we do flows out of our love relationship with Jesus, we create ample space in our worship settings for people to get beyond the words and music to actually sing to God and experience His manifest presence.

People who are desperately in love with Jesus are in a constant state of active and ongoing repentance from their sins. They overcome their insecurities and join God in His work of touching lives all around them. They let God lead in their lives, and it affects how they treat their co-workers, raise their children, and give their resources with generosity.

Kingdom Worship

Deep in theology of the Vineyard movement is our commitment to the Kingdom of God being in our midst, as Jesus taught. The Kingdom of God is where God's rule and reign are active, and as we worship, we are yielding ourselves to become vessels through which our King can impact the world He so loves (Jn. 3:16).

Our worship practices are rooted in our theology of the Kingdom of God. Jesus talked about the Kingdom of God in two distinct ways. Sometimes, it seemed like the Kingdom of God was something that was already present in His ministry. This is the Kingdom *now*. Sometimes, it seemed like the Kingdom of God was something that was yet to come. This is the Kingdom *not yet*.

The Vineyard has always believed that healthy Kingdom worship recognizes this tension. At times, we experience the Kingdom as a present reality. The sick are healed. Justice comes for the oppressed. People struggling with mental illness are set free.

At other times, the Kingdom does not come fully in the present. But we believe that one day, Jesus will return to make all things new – and in that day, all of our prayers for healing will be fully answered.

The Now And Not Yet In Worship

How does this view of God's Kingdom being *now* and *not yet* influence how we worship? The songs that come from the Vineyard reflect this theological tension we see in the teaching of Jesus.

In a time of worship in a Vineyard, we may sing songs that celebrate God's Kingdom being here, now, and breaking into our midst. These songs are filled with faith, joy, and celebration of God's present, miraculous, saving work among us. God heals. God delivers. God reigns. These kinds of lyrics are in many of our songs, and are true.

In other worship songs, however, you will notice a different tone. These songs are also filled with faith, yet they give space for our longing for God in a broken world to be expressed. We live in this reality – some people are prayed for, and are not healed.

Devastation occurs due to earthquakes, disease, suicide – and our hearts break. Our own sin sometimes gets the better of us, and we must turn our hearts to repentance.

Our songwriters care for this side of the Kingdom *not yet* being expressed in our lyrics and approach to worship. Among our thousands of songs are lyrics like "Come, let us sing for joy!" as well as "Broken, I run to You for Your arms are open wide...."

These kinds of songs stand side by side in our catalog, reflecting both of these realities of the Kingdom. All are songs of worship, reflecting the diversity of the book of Psalms with its exuberant words of praise and contrasting cries of desperation.

Some songs give us permission to shout with rambunctious joy at all God is doing in the world.

Other songs give us permission to express longing, offer Jesus our pain, repent of sin, surrender our hardened hearts, and cry out to God for the oil of His mercy to comfort us.

While this tension can be difficult to navigate, we in the Vineyard choose to hold the "radical middle" – as we worship a God who is present among us, in times of both joy and sorrow.

Worship Stirs Worship

In response to God's initiative, we value the life-changing power of the experience of His presence.

So, experience-based worship is the central activity of all that we do in the Vineyard. It is worship that causes all else that we do to become an act of worship.

OUR VALUES IN WORSHIP

We Are A Worship Movement

The Vineyard Movement is, at its very roots, a *worship* movement.

Our vision of the fulfilled life is found in John 4:23-24, *"Yet a time is coming and has now come when the true worshippers will worship the Father in the Spirit and in truth, for they are the kind of worshippers the Father seeks. God is spirit, and his worshippers must worship in the Spirit and in truth."*

If God is always seeking honesty and authenticity, what "in truth" may mean in the passage above, then there is no aspect of life – no struggle, no victory, no challenge – that He will not use to open our hearts to His love.

THE VINEYARD DNA

Worship – Our Highest Priority

As John Wimber said in 1992, "We in the Vineyard have, from the very outset of our ministry, made worship our highest priority, believing that it is God's desire that we become, first, worshippers of God." For this reason, we value both a vision of worship that permeates every aspect of lives, as well as the gathered worship experiences that energize us and empower us as we say, "I love you, O Lord, my strength" (Ps. 81:1) in song.

In order to create worship environments that open the heart to God's love in a give-and-receive posture, certain values shape our approach to gathered worship.

Here are just a few of our values in worship:

We value intimacy with God, believing that making ourselves vulnerable to God's Spirit as He has made Himself vulnerable to us (Phil. 2:5-11) is vital to knowing God as He desires to be known.

We value accessibility in our worship environments, seeking to create an open path for every person, of every age and background, to meet with God.

We value integrity in our worship lifestyle, desiring for our lives to match the lyrics we sing – whether they be about caring for the poor, loving our neighbors, or joining God in His work.

We value cultural connection in our worship styles, appreciating that sounds and forms of music provide a bridge for the heart for different generations and people groups.

We value Kingdom expectation in our approach to worship leadership, believing that as we respond to God in song, His Spirit is with us to heal, deliver, and set us free – in the midst of worship.

These and other values shape both the content and style of our worship times in local churches. We value spiritual gifts, creativity, diversity, healing, prophecy, passion, caring for the poor, and other themes that all impact the way worship is uniquely expressed in our churches.

Worship Overflows In Mission

Because the Vineyard movement is committed to equipping the saints for the work of ministry in all arenas of society (Eph. 4:12-16), we see our worship experiences taking us beyond our church services.

Worship, in our understanding of the Gospel, is to overflow in *mission*. We are committed to an understanding of worship that recognizes that we meet with God within the four walls of our churches to remember our calling, be healed in His presence, and offer God the praise that is due Him. Yet that experience also trains our hearts to express Jesus' love to a waiting world.

To use a metaphor, we breathe in God's presence as we yield to Him in worship, then we breathe out in fruitful work that heals individuals and society at large. For this reason, you may hear Vineyard leaders talking about worship in a way that goes beyond what happens when we gather to sing in a church service.

You will hear about worship being expressed through the giving of substance from our resources, caring for the poor, serving those in distress, praying for those in our workplaces, planting churches, administering justice, furthering the life of the mind in scholarship, and extending the Kingdom of God in every nation and people group.

To be a worshipping people, for us, is to experience the love of God – then to carry that love with us into a desperate world.

A Fresh Wind Of Courage
To be worshippers of God means that we are learning to love what God loves, and to hate what God hates. God loves people, and so we serve others as an act of worship.

When we experience Christ's reality in worship, we are healed by God's love, refreshed by God's presence, and empowered by God's Spirit. Strengthened by God in worship, week after week after week, we receive a fresh wind of courage to go into all the world "making disciples of all nations" (Matt. 28:19).

God Is Eager To Be Experienced
Worship has always been one of the hallmarks of the Vineyard. Many people describe their first moment in the Vineyard as being the moment in which they encountered God through intimate worship singing.

Worshipping and experiencing God goes far beyond singing. In every moment of our lives, we seek to live in the presence of the Lord. At the same time, corporate singing is a precious part of what it means for us to be the people of the Kingdom. In these times the Kingdom of God breaks in, and we, in the presence of Jesus himself, are changed.

Bless you as you experience God's presence in worship. May the reality of His love for you renew you, restore you, and compel you to join His Kingdom mission.

THOUGHTS FROM WIMBER ON WORSHIP

The late John Wimber, founding leader of the Vineyard, was a songwriter as well as a pastor, church planter, and church renewal leader. His heart for worship has impacted church leaders around the world, and his influence on the worship practices of the contemporary church cannot be overstated.

Here are a few quotes from John about worship and its leadership.

"...We don't use worship for anything else but to worship God – not even emotion. People are emotional and that's fine, but we don't use anything to cause the work of the Holy Spirit. Let God be God and do what He wills...."

"...Thus worship has a two-fold aspect: communication with God through the basic means of singing and praying, and communication from God through teaching and preaching the word, prophecy, exhortation, etc. We lift Him up and exalt Him, and as a result are drawn into His presence where He speaks to us...."

"Worship is not about personality, temperament, personal limitations, church background, or comfort. It's about God."

"...I think it's important for our worship leaders in the Vineyard to know what they've been invited to. They lead us to the throne, but then they need to get out of the way. We're not there to worship them, so they need to point us to Jesus... period."

"Values affect what we think, and consequently, what we do. Our values are an intrinsic part of us, although we seldom think about them in a

conscious fashion. They determine the ideas, principles, and concepts a person or group can accept, assimilate, remember, and transfer. They can be fallible and must be constantly revised and reviewed in the light of Scripture."

"...Not only is it helpful to understand why and how we worship God, it is also helpful to understand what happens when we worship God. ...Keep in mind that as we pass through these phases we are headed toward one goal: intimacy with God. I define intimacy as belonging to, or revealing one's deepest nature to another (in this case to God), and it is marked by close association, presence, and contact...."

-JOHN WIMBER

[Quotes excerpted from *Why We Worship & The Phases Of The Heart*; *The Values Of A Worship Leader*; and John Wimber Facebook Page.]

CHAPTER 7
OUR VALUES

For the Vineyard, our values frame our purpose, our priorities, and where we will put our time, energy, and resources.

Our values give meaning to all that we do. They also drive our purpose, define what is central to us, position the Vineyard in the larger body of Christ, and remove ambiguity in mission.

Before we look at some of our central values, let's pause to consider the purpose of the Vineyard Movement, and our shared calling.

OUR JOURNEY TOGETHER

Who We Are
The Vineyard is a God-initiated, global movement of churches with the Kingdom of God as its theological center.

THE VINEYARD DNA

The Bible is our rule of faith and practice. Our desire is to know the Bible, do what it says, and experience the way of living it describes. We embrace a full range of Kingdom practices, from proclaiming the Good News of Jesus, to healing and deliverance, to ministry with the poor.

Vineyard churches embody a praxis that includes intimate worship, actively equipping ordinary people for ministry, responding to the initiative and leading of the Holy Spirit, and joining God's mission in the world.

What We Do

In light of this, we believe that God has called the Vineyard in its leadership structures to participate in the Kingdom of God as it moves forward by

- Providing pastoral care, vision, resources, and oversight to help local Vineyard churches fulfill their God-given calling.
- Envisioning and motivating pastors and leaders to join God's mission by multiplying churches around the world.
- Training and empowering current pastors to disciple, train, and send future leaders.

Where We Are Going

We will know we have succeeded in our mission when we see thousands of churches with Vineyard theology and practices multiplied around the world – led by pastors who are theologically, practically, and spiritually equipped to pursue their unique calling to "the greater glory of God and the well-being of people."

VINEYARD VALUES

This articulation of our purpose for existing leads us to the foundation for the values we hold dear – our theological center of the *Kingdom of God*.

The Vineyard is a God-initiated, global movement of churches committed to theology and practice of the Kingdom of God, rooted in the vision of the Hebrew prophets, and fulfilled in the life and ministry of Jesus of Nazareth.

Our Guiding Theological Center

We have been commissioned to proclaim the Good News of the Kingdom, bearing witness to the already and not yet of the Kingdom in words and deeds.

The Vineyard is a movement distinctively centered in a renewed understanding of the centrality of the Kingdom of God in biblical thought. We view the Kingdom of God as the overarching and integrating theme of the Bible.

From our beginnings, the Vineyard has been committed to the proclamation of the Kingdom of God and to bearing witness to the deeds of the Kingdom through healing (physical, emotional, and social), doing justice, and delivering those held captive by evil.

Since the Kingdom of God is the future reign of God breaking into the present through the life and ministry of Jesus, we are a forward-leaning movement emphasizing the ever-reforming nature of the Church engaging the world in love.

THE VINEYARD DNA

As a movement, then, the following values shape our shared life together in community, and the practices that express the following values in real time.

WE ARE A PEOPLE OF THE KINGDOM OF GOD WHO...

Partner With The Holy Spirit

The Vineyard story is driven by the reality that God eagerly desires us to experience His presence, and then to partner with Him in His work of showing His love to the world. We believe that the Holy Spirit distributes gifts among us, enabling us to encounter God's presence personally and corporately, and then to minister to the world around us in the power of the Spirit.

Because the Holy Spirit is active among us as God's people, and in the world around us, our job as Christians is to partner with the Spirit, giving God permission to move in our lives and gatherings. Allowing the Spirit to lead in our lives and in our churches is the first step toward experiencing the promised fruits of the Spirit (Gal. 5:22-23).

As communities of the Spirit, we are not simply implementing the best church strategies, trying to accomplish what is humanly possible. Rather, our mission involves praying and finding power from God Himself to accomplish what humans could never accomplish on their own. We pray for the sick, we confront injustice, and we seek to hear the voice of God on behalf of others.

Experience And Worship God

The Kingdom of God is not a geo-political territory, nor is it the people of God. Rather, the Kingdom of God is a dynamic realm. When one enters the Kingdom she/he experiences the dynamic reality which exists within the triune God – Father, Son, and Holy Spirit. This means that the experience of the Kingdom of God (and thus, the experience of God's presence) is central to our faith and Christian life.

God is eager to be known and experienced by all. We believe that God is searching for lost humanity in order to draw us into intimate relationship with Himself. In response to God's initiative, we value the life-changing power of the experience of His presence.

The primary place where that relationship is nurtured and developed is in the act of worship – both private and corporate. So, experience-based worship is the central activity of all that we do in the Vineyard. It is worship that causes all else that we do to become an act of worship.

We experience God's presence as a palpable reality when we worship. As we worship, we become increasingly sensitive and responsive to the Spirit's presence so that we can do as Jesus did: "See what the Father is doing," (John 5:19) and support His work with our lives.

The experience of God flowing out of a life of worship affects all aspects of our lives, so that all division between the secular and the sacred vanish. We believe that the Spirit distributes His gifts to us, resulting in prophecy, prayer languages, healing, miracles, and many other gifts as we joyfully experience His presence.

We value an approach to God's presence that is respectful both of God and of those we are with. We eschew hype and other efforts to manipulate either God's presence or the response of others to His presence. We distinguish between the Holy Spirit and the human response which shares in all the beauty and brokenness of our humanity.

We also believe that as we experience His presence through Christ by the Spirit we will be made more fully human and better reflections of the God-image that we were created to be.

Reconcile People With God And All Creation

Jesus is reconciling humans to God, to each other, and to the entire creation, breaking down divisions between Jew and Gentile, slave and free, male and female. Therefore, we are committed to becoming healing communities engaged in the work of reconciliation wherever sin and evil hold sway.

We seek to be diverse communities of hope that realize the power of the cross to reconcile what has been separated by sin. This requires us to move beyond our personal preferences to engage those who are perceived to be unlike us and to actively break down barriers of race, culture, gender, social class, and ethnicity.

We are convinced that the church – locally, nationally, and globally – is meant to be a diverse community precisely because Jesus is Lord over every nation, tribe, and tongue. We are not satisfied with the status quo when it doesn't reflect this Kingdom reality, but are eager to pray for the coming of God's Kingdom here and now and to realize this mark of the Kingdom in our midst.

Engage In Compassionate Ministry

We lean toward the lost, the poor, the outcast, and the outsider with the compassion of Jesus as sinners whose only standing before God is utterly dependent on the mercy of God. This mercy can only be truly received inasmuch as we are willing to give it away.

We believe that ministry in Jesus' name should be expressed in concrete ways through the local church. The poor are to be served as though serving Jesus Himself. This is one of the distinguishing characteristics of a church expressing the love of Christ in a local community.

In all forms of ministry, compassion is a hallmark of the One who was moved with compassion Himself in the face of human need. This being the age of grace and "the year of the Lord's favor" (Luke 4:19), compassion should constitute the leading edge of our service to God, each other, and a broken world. As such, we seek to avoid unauthorized judgments of others, realizing that we are all fellow sufferers and strugglers with the rest of humanity.

Pursue Culturally Relevant Mission In The World
The Church exists for the sake of those who are exiled from God. We are called to bring the Gospel of the Kingdom to every nook and cranny of creation, faithfully translating the message of Jesus into language and forms that are relevant to diverse peoples and cultures.

We seek to plant churches that are culturally relevant in a wide variety of settings locally and internationally. Each Vineyard church is encouraged to reach those in its community not already reached by existing churches.

To this end, we promote a creative, entrepreneurial, and innovative approach to ministry that is faithful to Jesus and expressive of His heart to reach those who are far away from God.

CHAPTER 8
OUR PRACTICES

We have all been given, by God Himself, the gift of one short hour on the earth. Deep in our bones, we know that people need to experience the overwhelming, transforming love of God.

We also know that we have the opportunity to participate with God in bringing His Good News to every last person who breathes air in our generation!

So what takes us off track from joining God in His all-important work of loving people to Himself? If we use the metaphor of a sailing ship, we can first understand what forces pull us off course in order to better understand the practices that keep us on course.

Keeping On Course With The Kingdom
The Kingdom of God is Jesus' favorite topic – He talks about it over

100 times in the Bible. The Kingdom is not a geographical place. Rather, the Kingdom of God is the realm in which God's good, perfect, kind, and generous will takes place.

Where the Kingdom of God is expressed, sins are forgiven, sicknesses are healed, outsiders become insiders, and injustice is overturned into justice. The Kingdom of God was here long before we were – and will be here after we pass on.

The Church, however, is different from the Kingdom. The Church is the community of people who follow Jesus. The purpose of the Church is to extend God's Kingdom into the world. Local expressions of the Church are not perfect places. They are made up of flawed people doing an imperfect (but usually well-intentioned) job of being the people that God wants them to be.

Theologian George Ladd wrote, "The Church therefore is not the Kingdom of God; God's Kingdom creates the Church and works in the world through the Church" (Ladd, *Gospel Of The Kingdom*, p. 117).

The Church exists to extend God's Kingdom – not the other way around. Putting the Church, or our local church, in front of the Kingdom – is like putting a cart in front of a horse.

The Difference Between The Kingdom & The Church
The Kingdom is God's work; the Church is people trying to get in on God's work! The Kingdom is where God's will is fully expressed; the Church is the people of God trying to do God's will. The Kingdom can never fail, but the Church often will. Therefore, one of the most important mandates on the Church is that we put the Kingdom first – in all of our teaching and practices.

This in no way undermines the value of the Church. The Church is the people of God, the dwelling place of the Spirit, the community formed and ruled by Jesus. The Church is the primary means by which Jesus extends His reign on earth. In the book of Ephesians, Paul says that *"God's purpose in all this was to use the church to display his wisdom in its rich variety to all the unseen rulers and authorities in the heavenly places"* (Eph. 3:10 NLT).

It is the Church that demonstrates God's rule and reign in the world.

How We Get Off Course
Church life gets off course when a church starts existing for its own sake, rather than existing to demonstrate God's love to the world. Few of us would say our church is off course, but we may have some blind spots that are slowly pulling us away from God's great priorities.

How can church congregations make sure that the Kingdom comes first, week in and week out? How can we keep ourselves from becoming self-centered communities? How can we do our best to see that God's love for the world comes first, and that the Church takes its rightful place as the community expressing God's heart of love for men, women, and children?

Essential Practices To Keep Us On Course
A few constant practices can keep us on course as individuals and churches. As the earliest disciples experienced, doing what Jesus invited us to do with Him can keep us on course with God's heart for the world. And what essential practices did Jesus do, and teach us to do, *over and over again*? We can summarize the essential practices of Kingdom people with these four words:

Evangelism.
Discipleship.
Leadership.
Diversity.

Or, in short form:

"EDLD – Do It Again."

Keeping these four essential practices in front of us as local churches, and as the Vineyard, will keep us from maintaining the institutions of our churches while accidentally losing sight of Kingdom ministry.

These activities are the non-negotiables of life with Jesus. He has never stopped doing the work of evangelism, discipling individuals, nurturing them as leaders, and reaching out to the least, the last, and the lost of every tribe, age, and language.

We will never outgrow the need for these essential practices to rise again and again to the top of our list of priorities. Not only will the Kingdom expand, but what we do as we "EDLD" others will keep us on track – and change our hearts in the process.

Let's explore the heart behind each of these practices, one by one.

EVANGELISM: SHARE THE GOOD NEWS

We talk about what we love. Evangelism is talking about the Good News that Jesus is the Lord of the universe, the Savior of humanity, and the Lover of each and every person that ever lived. Mark reports the inauguration of Jesus' ministry with this mini-sermon: *"'The time has come,' he announced. 'The kingdom of God has come near. Repent and believe the good news!'"* (Mark 1:15).

It is good, good news that Jesus loves every person in your reach – whether they believe it right now or not.

Meeting Jesus Is The Key To Life
In a world scarred by sin, guilt, shame, and confusion, there is no better news than the news that Jesus is King, that He is setting things right, forgiving sin and healing souls. On a personal level, you may remember the moment when a saving knowledge of Jesus erupted in your heart, and you were filled with a powerful awareness of God's love for you for the very first time.

But the gift of meeting Jesus doesn't stop there. For those who will believe in him, Jesus offers the invitation to be adopted into the family of God. The lonely are placed into a family that lasts forever, where the rich become brothers and sisters with the poor, where prejudices fall under the weight of God's mercy for us all, and where servanthood displaces power as the path to greatness.

What's more, those who know Jesus need not fear death, for they have the hope of eternal life – eternal life that isn't only in the future, but can begin now! We are offered the promise of a new creation – starting with a new identity as a child of God.

It would be unspeakable, having heard such Good News, having tasted of the benefits of the Kingdom – not to share it with others! It would be like having the light people need, but hiding it under a basket. It would be like salt that doesn't have any taste. It would be like a poor woman finding an endless supply of bread, but refusing to bring any to her family and friends!

Evangelism Takes Different Forms

A witness is someone who has seen and experienced something, and then reports it. In fact, it is illegal to tamper with a witness, or to train a witness. A witness simply "tells it as they experienced it."

We can make evangelism something strange and difficult, or we can just share what – and Who – we love. We can be *witnesses*. The Good News of God's love for individuals is to be both proclaimed and demonstrated. The people of Jesus have always been known for healing the sick, serving the poor, and caring for the needy.

Encounters with the power and presence of God can open a closed heart more quickly than many spoken words. And we demonstrate what it looks like when the Kingdom comes. We offer verbal witness, explaining what this new life is that we are demonstrating – a life that Jesus offers, through His death and resurrection, a new birth that comes by faith.

The first step of effective evangelism begins in our own hearts. It begins by experiencing the love of God so deeply that it oozes out of us. John exclaims in his first letter, *"See how very much our Father loves us, for he calls us His children, and that is what we are!"* (John 3:1 NLT).

Restoring A Loving Vision Of God

When religion goes wrong, we fail to see God as a generous, loving Father. We may begin to view Him as a harsh taskmaster, or a distant ruler. We may wonder why anyone else would be interested in relationship with such a being!

If this has happened to us, if our view of God is so dim that we don't have any desire to share Him with others, the proper response is not to beat ourselves up or feel guilty. Rather, it is to go to God to ask for refreshing from His Spirit. It is to go to our brothers and sisters to ask them to pray for us, that our eyes would be opened to the depth of God's love for us.

When our view of God is restored, when we've been healed and are full of the love of God, we will begin to naturally look for opportunities to share that Good News with others!

The biblical term for this activity is *witness*. Jesus tells us that we will be full of the Spirit, and will bear witness to the goodness of Jesus all over the world (Acts 1:8). We are witnesses, and we bear witness to what God has done.

Evangelism is not a program, nor is it the result of over-work. Evangelism is about the over-flow of a soul, full of the goodness of God, in the presence of another.

We Are Witnesses

Notice that we ourselves are not the saviors! We don't offer other people perfect love; we ourselves cannot forgive, heal, and deliver. We simply witness to the One who can. We offer our own story, the stories of Scripture, and prayer for the presence of the Spirit, Who will authenticate the message. Healthy evangelism puts all the pressure on God. We are simply witnesses of His goodness and power.

Jesus Himself recognizes that not all people will respond to the Good

News in the same way. In Matthew 13, He tells the story of a farmer who sows seed – a metaphor for the proclamation of the Gospel. It is understood that not all the seed will produce fruit – some will fall on a road, and some will be choked out by thorns or rocks. Our job is simply to witness to the love and power of God, knowing that some will respond, and some will not. This should neither shock nor disappoint us.

Of course, over time, we will develop increasingly effective methods for sharing the Good News. Churches will organize various kinds of outreach, we will get more skilled at telling our stories, and we will become more courageous at offering prayer or prophetic insight to others.

And some people, by the grace of God, will seem to be more fruitful than others in evangelism. That is wonderful, but sometimes we use this as an excuse to withhold sharing about Jesus' love for us and others.

We are all called to simply bear witness to the world around us that Jesus offers overwhelming love to all people – and especially to the person in front of us.

When we are witnesses to others of His love – then we do it again, with every opportunity God brings our way.

DISCIPLESHIP: HELP CHRISTIANS GROW

What happens once a person comes to faith in Jesus? How does that person grow in maturity, in faith, and in love? Does it happen automatically? Does he or she immediately sin less, love more, discover gifts, and walk in victory?

Making Disciples Is Intentional

The Bible's answer to these questions is "No." Every new Christian has a process of healing and growth to enter into that involves studying the Scriptures, learning to pray, and embracing one's new identity as a child of God. We call this process *discipleship*.

A new believer must be trained to become an apprentice of Jesus, and he or she usually needs someone to walk alongside them in that growth process.

As Christians, we are mandated to go into all the world, and to make disciples by teaching people how to act, think, and love like Jesus in their everyday lives. Discipleship is a relational process by which people help one another become more like Christ. It is not accidental nor automatic. It is *intentional*.

Go And Make Disciples

If we practice evangelism, the next logical step is to begin to disciple those who have come to faith. To disciple others is an act of simple obedience to Jesus' command in Matthew 28 – *"Therefore go and make disciples of all nations, baptizing them in the name of the Father and of the Son and of the Holy Spirit, and teaching them to obey everything I have commanded you"* (Matt. 28:19-20a).

In other words, people who give their lives to Jesus must be taught to obey Jesus' teachings. Old habits die hard, and Jesus' call to surrender runs up against our lifetime habit of taking care of #1 – ourselves! Becoming like Jesus doesn't just happen; people discipling

140

people produces the fruit of healthy, mature Christians – and healthy, mature churches.

Leaders in the Church of Jesus must come to the realization that discipleship is our task. It is not something we can simply delegate to others, or hope that people will discover on their own. Rather, we must come to terms with the fact that Jesus has commanded us to make disciples.

Am I Discipling Others?

One way we can assess how we are doing in discipleship is to ask a simple question: "Does our name come up in someone else's story of spiritual growth?" Most people are discipled by committee! If we tell the story of how we have grown in Christ, we name names. Parents, relatives, neighbors, youth leaders, pastors, small group leaders, mentors, friends, prayer partners, and on and on – these are the names that show up in people's stories. If someone you know told his or her story of discipleship, would your name be spoken?

We can ask ourselves, "Who am I involved with right now in such a way that I am reasonably sure my name would come up in one of their testimonies?" Don't be falsely humble, but don't lie to yourself either! This is a crucial question. We can become so busy with the work of maintaining church structures that we lose track of the command from Jesus to make disciples.

If our answer is that we are not involved in the intentional discipleship of Christians, then we need to deal with this reality. One way to do this is to simply write down our schedule for a given week. If we are not discipling others in that schedule, then we should ask what we are doing with our time. What are we so busy doing that we aren't taking time to invest in the growth of others? This need not be a shaming experience at all. It is simply a way of revealing our reality, and adjusting our life to reflect the values of God's Kingdom in our weekly choices.

How Do We Disciple Others?
The answer to this question is as varied as are human beings. We don't generally need to ask someone "Would you like me to disciple you?" Choosing to disciple is simply a matter of taking note of the people around you and asking yourself what you could do to help them grow toward God.

The first step of discipleship is often listening – a double listening to others and to God. If you've never taken a class or read a book on effective listening, you may want to do so as soon as possible. Listening is probably the most important part of discipleship. If we don't listen, we'll probably just project our lives onto other people. That is not love, nor is it the foundation for healthy relationships.

After a lot of listening, discipleship also involves the willingness to challenge others. Depending on their personality, this might be a gentle nudge, or it may involve a fairly direct confrontation of a behavior.

Discipleship is about helping another person grow in becoming like Christ. For that reason, discipleship needs to involve the Bible, and helping the other person apply the lessons of Scripture to daily life in the real world.

The Outcome Of Real Discipleship

The outcome of discipleship is a person knowing he or she is deeply loved by God, turning to Christ in times of success and struggle, and then turning one's energies toward lavishly offering Jesus' love to others through evangelism and discipleship.

In other words, we evangelize and disciple again and again. Then the people we evangelize and disciple do the same thing for others – again and again over their lifetimes.

LEADERSHIP: MULTIPLY LEADERS

As disciples grow, they are called to begin to serve others more effectively. Some become leaders of others in that process. In the Kingdom of God, leadership is accomplished by serving others. The best leaders are the best servants. We are called to help disciples become true servant leaders in all arenas of their lives.

Two Truths About Leadership

Before we walk through six steps that can help us build some disciples to be leaders, we need to emphasize two very important truths about leadership.

The first we've already stated: leadership is servanthood. Leadership is not about ordering others around or enjoying the feeling of power. Leaders exist to serve others (Luke 22:25-27).

The second truth about leadership is that leadership is about action, not position or titles. Leaders don't really care what others call them. They simply take the actions God has led them to take.

If people seek leadership out of pride, or to impress others, they are not yet mature enough to be leaders. We should go back to the step of discipleship, and ask God how we can help them grow in humility and servanthood. It can be tempting to make people into leaders too soon.

On the other hand, it can also be tempting to never call people into leadership. We may think that we are simply supposed to do everything ourselves. We may be clinging to our own leadership platform and find it difficult to give that platform away to another. Or we may think that we need to wait until people are perfectly mature. People don't have to be perfect to be leaders – they simply need to be open and humble enough to let God use them.

IRTDMN – A Leadership Multiplication Process

IRTDMN is a series of letters that provides a memorable way to think about our process of developing leaders. Each letter represents a vital step in the process of helping a disciple become a leader of others, and then become a developer of other leaders.

I – *The first step of leadership development is to **identify** a leader.*

How do we identify a leader? The first step is to pray and ask God to show us whom we are to develop as a leader. What does your heart tell you? Who do you sense God's hand is on to show others what it means to be a disciple? The second is to simply observe people. Who seems to be influential? Who is willing to take initiative?

Try putting a board game on a table in the middle of a social event to see who starts the game! Or you may notice that one person always arrives early and stays late, or asks more questions with more hunger than anyone else in the group. That person could be a spiritual leader in the making.

144

As you observe the followers of Jesus in your sphere of relationships, look for the traits of humility, servanthood, faithfulness, availability, and teachability. These are the marks of a leader ready to fly.

R – *The second step is to **recruit** the leader.*

We must develop an idea of what we'd like the person to do, and then ask them to do it. Sometimes we aren't clear enough on what it is we want someone to do. They can become confused about what they are being asked to do, and may pull away from leading. Clarity can help a person stay in the growth process that is leadership.

You may find a person to be a bit reticent to step into a leadership role. Encourage them with the fact that you believe in them, that they are loved by God, and that they are called to use their gifts to serve others. Don't pressure them to become leaders, but don't be afraid to encourage them to take a risk and lead.

T – *The third step is to **train** the leader.*

This may or may not involve a class or some curriculum, but even if it does, that isn't the main part of training. The main part of training is what we call the "discipleship loop."

The discipleship loop has four parts. First, we lead while the new leader watches. Second, they lead while we observe. Third, they lead on their own, and we check in on them to ask how they are doing. Fourth, they recruit someone to do that leadership task, and begin the process of training them.

By the time the discipleship loop is complete, both you and the leader you trained are now training others. That is where the multiplication begins.

D – *The fourth step is to **deploy** the leader.*

Let them go lead. This involves risk on the part of the new leader and the person developing them. It's okay if things don't go perfectly. All leaders take time to grow.

One really important part of this step is to get beyond the fear of people making mistakes. Mistakes are one of the most underrated forms of spiritual growth. If new leaders make mistakes, just encourage them to try again. Usually they will do fine the second time around.

M – *The fifth step is important – we **monitor** the new leader.*

This doesn't mean hovering over them or controlling them. It means that we don't simply abandon them; we have some way of checking in on them to see how they're doing.

One way we do this is to simply ask them how their leadership task is going. Another way to monitor is to ask the people they are leading how they think the endeavor is going, and how they think the leader is doing. Sometimes we will get more honest input this way.

N – *The final step of leadership development is to **nurture** the leader.*

The Kingdom of God is about community and relationship, not lone rangers. All of us need people in our lives to hold us accountable, and to encourage us when we are discouraged.

The nurture step is like getting an oil change. You can ignore the need for an oil change for a while, and things might seem to be fine with your car. But ignore it for too long – and things will break down. It's the same with leaders. They can go without nurture for a bit, but if they never receive it, they'll become tired and burnt out.

Evangelize, disciple, and *develop leaders* – then *do it again*.

Now there is one more step to which we need to attend, and which we often miss due to another blind spot – our background and culture.

DIVERSITY: REACH OUT TO THOSE DIFFERENT FROM YOU

Diversity isn't a *step* in the EDLD process in the same way that evangelism, discipleship, and leadership development are. Rather, diversity is a *value* that must permeate the entire process. If it doesn't, we will, by our very natures, only evangelize, disciple, and multiply leaders who are naturally part of our own social group.

Without the value of diversity in us and in our community, we will miss one of the greatest of Kingdom truths – that God loves people who are men, women, and children, from every race and nation, and in every stage of life. Everyone one of them is made in His image!

The Kingdom of God is not an old boys' or girls' club. It is not just for young people, nor is it just for old people, male people, female people, people with our skin color, or people who speak our language.

THE VINEYARD DNA

The Kingdom of God is for everyone.

We need men and women, children and youth, people from many ethnic backgrounds, and people of many languages to share the Gospel, disciple, train leaders, and love people into wholeness in Christ!

That is how the Kingdom of God has advanced through history, and how the Church has grown for millennia. When Paul was told in a dream to go to Macedonia in Acts 16, he was being called by God to risk loving others who were not in his immediate, familiar environment.

According to the powerful stories in the book of Acts, diversity in our evangelism, discipleship, and leadership multiplication matters to God – and He calls us out of our comfort zones to become a part of another's story.

Why Does Diversity Matter?
Does it matter if we are a diverse community? At times, the Church has seemed to think that it doesn't matter. At these times, we have been lulled into thinking that it is probably fine if churches are just full of people who think, act, and look the same.

Certainly churches might grow a bit faster this way – if they simply target the people they already know how to reach!

However, if we really want to grow Jesus' Church then we know, deep down, this kind of attitude is simply not okay. We must remember that the Kingdom is more important than the Church, and that healthy churches are committed to the Kingdom advancing above their own agendas. Advancing God's Kingdom means we must enter the story of those with whom we would not normally associate.

Healthy Christians are courageous in this way, and look for diversity in those they evangelize, disciple, and train to be leaders. The Kingdom has always been a diverse reality. We see this in the genealogy of Jesus in Matthew 1. Matthew goes out of the way to show that Jesus had a multicultural background! Jesus didn't just stick with the Jews – He evangelized Samaritans and Gentiles.

He didn't just command His disciples to reach people who were already a part of their tribe – He called them to Jerusalem, but also to Judea, to Samaria, and to the ends of the earth!

At the birth of the Church, when the Spirit was poured out (Acts 2), God gave gifts to people enabling them to speak of His wonders in many different languages. In John's vision of the fulfillment of the Kingdom in the heavenly throne room, there are multitudes from every tribe and nation. The greatest church planter in the early church, Paul, made it very clear that he wanted to plant multiethnic churches, even if others resisted him.

Beyond The Familiar

One fascinating narrative happens when the apostle Peter is called to reach one of the first gentile converts in Acts 10. Initially Peter resists – he is not comfortable sharing Christ with a Roman soldier. He was much more comfortable staying with his own kind of people.

But the Spirit showed him that the Roman soldier Cornelius was worthy of hearing about Jesus – about the Gospel of theKingdom –

and was ready to receive salvation. So Peter obeyed, and the Church began to fulfill the mission of being a multiethnic expression of the Kingdom of God.

In the Vineyard, those who are already in the *in-crowd* can easily get their cultural needs met. It can feel so comfortable to us that we don't even realize we may not be as good at helping people from other cultures or classes get their needs met. We need to let God change us so that we don't always minister to others in a way that is always comfortable to us and our culture.

Many Cultures & Ages Get To Play

In God's Kingdom, no single culture gets to be on home base all the time! At times, we should all sing songs we don't know yet, or hear preaching that is different from what we're used to. We might find that our political or social assumptions get upset by others who are different from us. But this is all for the good – diversity helps us grow.

Much of the responsibility for growing in diversity lies with what is called the *dominant* culture. People of the dominant culture must learn to listen and learn to be welcoming – not just open.

We must be willing to accept that some of our assumptions might be wrong, and that learning to operate cross culturally, while difficult, brings us all into a much richer experience of God's Kingdom.

And there are so many cultures in God's creation that once we have learned one, we can always find another – and *do it again!*

ESSENTIAL PRACTICES OF THE VINEYARD - A SUMMARY

Evangelism, Discipleship, Leadership, and Diversity. These four essential practices of Kingdom people will keep you and I, as well as our churches, on course with God's advancing Kingdom. As you read through each of these sections below, ask God again, "How can I join You in seeing Your love extended to others in my reach through each one of these practices?"

Then, take a risk, and "do it again."

Evangelism: Share The Good News
Share the good news about Jesus with people who don't know him yet. Invite them into the Kingdom reality in the power of the Spirit. And don't just share with people of your own culture, learn to share the Good News of God's love in other cultures as well. Then do it again.

Discipleship: Help Christians Grow
Help those new believers grow in Christ. Listen to them and challenge them. Teach them how the Scriptures apply to their daily lives, and what it means to become like Jesus. Learn how their culture operates so that you can be more effective at helping them grow in their soil. Then do it again.

Leadership: Multiply Leaders
Develop and release new leaders in the church. Look for those God's hand is on to lead among those who are being discipled. Apply the IRTDMN process to each person, and give them the space to risk with your support around them. Then do it again.

Diversity: Reach Out To Those Different From You
Don't just release the same kind of leaders over and over – look for ways to release different generations, genders, and ethnicities into leadership. Revel in the diversity of people, and find ways for them to express that uniqueness as they follow Christ. Then do it again.

Put the Kingdom first in your life and that of your church. Then "EDLD" others again and again – until the day Christ returns and the Kingdom comes in all its fullness.

CHAPTER 9
TOWARD OUR FUTURE

The Vineyard is moving into its second generation of ministry. Our great hope is that God will enable us to hold onto much of what we have cherished for the past decades, then continue to add fresh wisdom and revelation to it.

As we move forward, we as Vineyard churches seek to be *worshipping communities, healing communities, biblical communities, outward communities, healthy communities, multiplying communities*, and *Spirit-led communities*.

Worshipping Communities

Vineyard churches have long been known for their worship music. Worship is more than music, but times of singing have been a cornerstone of Vineyard practice since our roots in 1970s Southern California. Early Vineyard worship was instrumental in transforming worship styles in churches all over the world.

THE VINEYARD DNA

One growing emphasis in Vineyard worship is homegrown music. Rather than simply using nationally produced and distributed songs, local congregations are increasingly developing their own musical liturgies.

Many of the shared songs of our movement come from these local expressions, rather than being handed down from a central office. This trend reflects our value for simple, authentic expression over any kind of hype or pretension.

Our worship practices are rooted in theology of the Kingdom of God. On one hand, the secular culture around us is capable of producing art full of common grace and beauty. At the same time, much of secular art declares that sex, money, and power are the true kings of the world.

Our worship expression seeks to tell an alternative story – that sex, money, and power have their places, but Christ is the true King. This is what our congregations declare each week when they gather together to sing the praises of the Creator and Lord of the universe.

Healing Communities

One of the hallmarks of the Vineyard movement from the beginning has been an emphasis on healing. The gospel records in the Bible tell us that Jesus and the earliest Christians were known for miraculous healings. In our post-enlightenment culture, it can be challenging to take this emphasis seriously. But from the beginning, the Vineyard has been more committed to Scripture than to current cultural norms.

As a result, we have always prayed faithfully for the sick – in our church services, in small groups, and in the everyday workplaces and neighborhoods we inhabit. We do not always see the sick healed, but we believe that every faith-filled act of prayer puts a deposit of love into the person who is suffering. And we have testimonies from every corner of the earth that, at times, the Kingdom of God does break through with power to heal those who are sick.

We do not only seek to heal bodies, but also to heal souls. Many come to our churches wounded by addictions, abuse, and other internal pain. Vineyard churches always seek to be a hospital for broken souls: a place where masks can come off, where pain can be expressed, and where healing can be found.

As our movement grows, we have seen that the healing of Jesus extends beyond individuals to society at large. Vineyard people care about racism, about environmental issues, about racial injustice, about sexual trafficking and exploitation.

All these efforts are rooted in our theology of the Kingdom of God. Jesus talked about the Kingdom of God more than any other topic. He talked about it in two ways. Sometimes, it seemed like the Kingdom of God was something that was already present in his ministry. Sometimes, it seemed like the Kingdom of God was something that was yet to come.

The Vineyard has always believed that healthy Kingdom ministry flows out of living in this tension. At times, we experience the Kingdom as a present reality. The sick are healed. Justice comes for the oppressed. People struggling with mental illness are set free. At other times, the Kingdom does not come in the present. But we believe that one day, Jesus will return to make all things new – and in that day, all of our prayers for healing will be fully answered.

THE VINEYARD DNA

Biblical Communities

Vineyard churches believe God has revealed Himself to us in the Scriptures. We are committed to careful study and interpretation of the Bible, and to faithful preaching of its message. We live under the authority of the Bible. And at times we can feel the tension in trying to live under its authority. Our experience, or the culture around us, can make trusting the Scriptures hard to do. But this is the nature of faith: to hold onto its authority even when it is extremely difficult.

At the same time, we do not see the study of the Bible as an end in itself. Early Vineyard teachers would often remind us, "Don't eat the menu." In other words, the Scriptures are to lead us into personal relationship with God. Studying the Bible fundamentally requires response and obedience to the Person the Bible is written about. The Scriptures lead us to worship God, to pray for the sick, to care for the poor, and to live in community.

One story from the life of John Wimber illustrates this point powerfully. Wimber had been a well-known musician with no experience of Christ or the Church. He had a powerful conversion through the witness of a close friend. Soon afterward, he visited a church for the first time. After a particularly dry time of singing and preaching, the service ended. Wimber turned to his friend and asked, "When do we get to do the stuff? You know, the stuff I read about in the Bible?"

Back then, John Wimber unwittingly pointed out what our relationship to the Bible could be. We always try to live deeply submitted to its living authority, and we want to put into practice the kind of dynamic relationship with God that is modeled right on the pages.

Outward Communities

A common saying in Vineyard circles is: "The local church is the only institution that exists primarily for those who aren't yet members." Our churches are not *holy huddles*, fearfully avoiding infection from the culture around us. Rather, we are outposts of the Kingdom of God, seeking to bring hope and help from Jesus to anyone who wants it.

We are evangelistic communities: we proclaim that in Jesus Christ there is forgiveness and hope for anyone who will put their faith in him. Evangelism in the Vineyard takes many forms. The Gospel is proclaimed in public worship services, Alpha courses, by street teams, in neighborhood Bible studies, and at dozens of other venues. We believe the greatest news anyone can hear is that there is a loving God who is longing for relationship with every human being.

We are concerned with the spiritual needs of our cities as well as their practical needs. Vineyard churches offer hundreds of creative acts of service in communities. Churches offer ESL programs, food shelves, after-school programs, housing programs, medical, dental, and legal services, among other forms of care. One prayer many Vineyard pastors pray is that we would be congregations our cities would deeply miss if we were ever to leave.

For us, being on mission is not isolated from our other activities. We believe our friends and neighbors need to offer worship to the living God. We believe their bodies and souls need healing. We believe they need to learn and practice the words of the Bible.

So, in many ways, mission ties together much of what we do in our churches. As one Vineyard leader put it, "the Church of Jesus is the hope of the world."

THE VINEYARD DNA

Healthy Communities

Vineyard leader Phil Strout may be best known for his famous question, "How is your soul?" It's a question we all need to hear. We are very aware that Christian leaders have not always been healthy people. In fact, many people who come into our churches have been wounded by unhealthy Christian leaders. Therefore, we are committed to being churches who practice emotional health.

The primary way we maintain health is through relationships with one another. All over the nation, small groups of Vineyard pastors meet on a regular basis for prayer, for soul care, and to share one another's burdens. Vineyard congregations often support one another financially or create service teams to help meet one another's needs.

We have also had an increasing emphasis on programs to help our leaders grow in more intentional ways. We sponsor conferences, retreats, and training sessions that help our members, leaders, and pastors learn to live lives of spiritual health. Isolated, overworked leaders can bring spiritual poison into a movement. We seek the opposite: healthy, well-connected, spiritually vibrant leaders who take our movement into the future.

Seeking to have healthy souls ties together many of the other themes of the Vineyard. Learning to live in the *already* and *not yet* of the Kingdom is crucial to our health – otherwise we live in endless disappointment or in unhealthy false triumphalism.

Lives of worship and outward focus keep our souls from turning dangerously inward, falling into narcissistic despair. Lives focused on the healthy balance of Scripture help us deal with the ongoing day-to-day stresses and struggles common to all humans.

Multiplying Communities

The apostle Paul is perhaps the best-known early Christian. He was a preacher, evangelist, author, and church planter. He launched new congregations in dozens of cities all over the Roman empire, in Greece, Turkey, Italy, and many other places. Few people have influenced the history of the Church more than Paul.

And yet, none of the congregations that Paul launched 2,000 years ago exist today. Certainly most of our churches would in some way trace their ancestry back to those early gatherings. But for the Christian movement to go forward, it's necessary to continually launch new congregations, for new generations, in new cultures.

The Vineyard started as a church-planting movement. Most Vineyard churches exist because an individual or team left an existing Vineyard, went to a new location, and started a new congregation. This process takes risk, sacrifice, and hard work. But the end result is a healthy congregation, expressing the Kingdom of God in fresh new ways.

We are committed to planting hundreds of new churches domestically and thousands more internationally in the coming years. This commitment involves a growing number of partnerships and strategies that require the investment of significant resources.

As a Vineyard leader often says: "We all eat fruit from trees we did not plant."

Planting new churches requires faith that if we invest ourselves for the sake of others, God will meet our needs as well.

THE VINEYARD DNA

Spirit-led Communities

A key verse in the history of the Vineyard is John 5:19:

"Jesus gave them this answer: 'Very truly I tell you, the Son can do nothing by himself; he can do only what he sees his Father doing, because whatever the Father does the Son also does.'"

We believe Jesus modeled deep dependence on God His Father, and we also ought to do only what we see the Father doing. For this reason, we have always tried to stay flexible and open to the voice of God, and we want to see what he is doing. We have built institutions, but we have also been willing to change course and direction as the Lord has led.

As we move into the future, staying focused on this reality is key. The Vineyard has never been about a human strategy or idea. We make plans, as the Scriptures model for us – but those plans are always subject to the voice of God. We believe God has spoken through the Bible and that He continues to speak to us today, in visions and prophecies and words of knowledge. We hear God in our time alone with Him and in public settings where we ask Him to speak to us.

Doing church this way is risky. We have always believed that faith is spelled R-I-S-K. At times, it can be tempting simply to come up with a really smart strategy on our own, rather than to move forward in a way that depends on the action and reality of a living God.

Moving forward in obedience to the Father is the essence of who the Vineyard desires to be – now and into the future.

ADDENDUM
THE 5 STEP PRAYER MODEL

As was stated earlier in this book, one of the most important distinctives of the Vineyard movement is captured in a simple, four-word phrase: "Everyone gets to play."

Coined by our founder John Wimber, and based on his understanding of the New Testament call to equip the saints for the work of ministry (Eph. 4:12), this phrase set the stage for the unique Vineyard approach to compassionately praying for others. It is the central prayer model for ministry in Vineyard churches – the *5 Step Prayer Model*.

John believed that every man, woman, and child who is willing to be used by God can learn to hear His voice. As we learn to hear God's voice, we can be led by the Spirit as we minister to others through personal prayer – rather than relying on our own limited experience or insight.

Wimber also taught that any person can cultivate one's ability to hear God's voice over time and through experience, thereby increasing our opportunities to partner with Christ in seeing lives changed, bodies healed, emotions restored to health, and people experiencing the radical, personal love that God uniquely has for them.

Wimber was recognized by the Church of the 20th and 21st centuries, across the world, for his healing ministry. He was known particularly for his low-hype, thoughtful, practical, authoritative, and matter-of-fact approach to operating in the gifts of the Spirit.

The Vineyard grew, in part, as God used John powerfully in the ministry of healing. It became normal to hear testimonies of many who experienced physical, emotional, and mental healing in connection with John's ministry. In his eyes, however, it was God doing the healing – not him – and God wanted every Christian engaged in praying for others.

John resisted the notion that some of us are called to be spiritual superstars, while others are just ordinary Christians. He was passionate about teaching believers to 'do the stuff' of ministry, offering practical approaches to prayer that de-mystified spiritual experience and power ministry. John knew that if ordinary folks learned how to allow the Holy Spirit to guide their prayers for others, Jesus would be made famous around the globe.

In his vital work on the topic, *Power Healing*, John wrote these words: "...Shortly after I saw my first healing, I asked myself, 'Is it possible to develop a model for healing from which large numbers of Christians may be trained to heal the sick?' I thought the answer was yes and became committed to developing that model" (*Power Healing*, p. 169).

THE VINEYARD DNA

This chapter captures the essence of Wimber and the Vineyard's approach to praying for others for all forms of healing, and is designed to be a tool of ministry in your hands as you learn how to effectively pray for others. The principles in these pages are backed by thousands of stories of miraculous encounters, physical healings, emotional transformations, remarkable acts of forgiveness, revelatory moments, demonic deliverances, and restorations of myriad lives to "the joy of the Lord" (Neh. 8:10b).

While the principles in this booklet often speak directly to prayer for physical healing, they apply to any prayer ministry situation we find ourselves in. It is our hope this approach will serve you and your community as you pray, with effectiveness and long-term fruit, for the people that God so loves (John 3:16).

PRAY FOR A THOUSAND PEOPLE, THEN WE'LL TALK

John Wimber's healing conferences and teaching impacted thousands of Christians around the world in the 20th century. He noted once that he would receive cards or letters after someone had heard him teach that would say something to the effect of, "I went home and prayed for somebody – and it didn't work." John would laugh and reply, "Why don't you pray for a thousand somebodies, and then let's talk."

The *5 Step Prayer Model* is not a scientific formula, fool-proof methodology, or magical incantation. Rather, it is an intentional way of praying for others, from a posture of listening to the Holy Spirit, that provides a track to run on for those desiring to see God move in power as they pray.

While physical healing is often the focus of prayer ministry, in its essence the *5 Step Prayer Model* is a relational, interactive way of praying for others as we listen to the Holy Spirit – a process that begins and ends with mercy toward the person requesting prayer, and that seeks both God's will and God's best for the person being prayed for. It is also relational in the sense that we are leaning heavily on our intimate relationship with God as we pray for someone, welcoming Him to speak insights into our hearts or minds that would directly impact the person being prayed for.

Vineyard churches around the world have a reputation for being places where compassionate, Spirit-guided prayer ministry can be received. For us, prayer ministry can happen in a church service, in a mechanic's garage, in a hospital room, or over a backyard fence.

"The five-step procedure may be used any time and in any place: in hotels, at neighbors' homes, on airplanes, at the office, and, of course, in church gatherings. I have been in casual conversation with people, even with complete strangers, who mention some physical condition, and I ask, 'May I pray for you?' Rarely do they decline healing prayer, even if they are not Christians. I then confidently pray for them by following the five-step method" (Wimber, *Power Healing*).

The basis for the approach in the following pages is the model of Jesus as He ministered to the sick. It also draws on Wimber's experience as he witnessed thousands of people encounter God's love through signs, wonders, and dramatic healings. Over time, and with practice, this way of praying for people is meant to become internalized. As we begin to see patterns when we pray for certain types of people or issues, we grow in our ability to hear God's voice as we are praying.

THE VINEYARD DNA

We may begin to experience the Holy Spirit giving us spiritual gifts as we pray. What we thought in the past were random impressions, we actually learn are gifts of revelation from God! We may begin to see people physically or emotionally healed, or at the very least leaving a time of prayer with a deposit of God's love in their heart.

Wimber once said that the worst thing we can do is rely on our past experience when praying for another. Each individual has a unique story, and God has something creative He wants to do. This keeps us humble, attentive, and ready to obey God as He leads us in praying for others.

THE 5 STEP PRAYER MODEL

Here are the five steps in the prayer model, designed to help you hear God's voice in prayer, to pray for the sick, and to minister compassionately to those in need.

STEP 1: THE INTERVIEW
Introduce yourself, then ask, "How can I pray for you?" or "Where does it hurt?"

In this first step, we introduce ourselves to the person, and ask the questions "How can I pray for you?" or "Where does it hurt?"

This is not a medical interview or a counseling session, but rather an opportunity to listen as we assess the person's situation and need. This step ensures that the person feels valued, and gives us an opportunity to listen to God and the individual before any prayer begins. It also enables us to hear how the person perceives his or her condition before jumping to any conclusions.

According to Wimber, we are listening to the person on two levels at this point. On a natural (empirical) level, we are hearing the request. On a supernatural level, we are listening simultaneously for God to speak to us about the person and/or the situation. Based on what we are seeing and hearing, as well as on past patterns we may recognize from praying for similar types of people or conditions, we can begin to assess how God might be leading us to pray.

However, we must not be dependent on our past experiences, but rather on God. Even as a person is speaking, the Holy Spirit may begin to give you pictures, scriptures, or other insights. In this case, it is not always necessary to have the person continue. Go right to prayer, as God may have another agenda that He wants to see fulfilled.

As we become increasingly sensitive and responsive to the Spirit's presence over years of practice (Wimber suggested 40 or 50 years to start!), we become open for the Spirit to give us spiritual gifts for ministry. During the interview, He may want to plant in our minds scriptures, words of knowledge (things we could not have otherwise known), or images (pictures illustrating something God is revealing).

We take our time, are quiet, and listen. Our dependence is on God to make something happen, not on ourselves. He wants to do something beautiful and creative in this person, and loves to use us in the process. Wimber would say, "It's more important to know what kind of person has a bug rather than what kind of bug has a person."

In other words, God may want to touch something in the person's life other than the illness or topic of the prayer request! Be open to the Spirit's guidance. If you have no clue what to pray after the interview, then be honest; don't fake it or put on a spiritual persona. Maintain your integrity, and if necessary, just pray for God to bless the person.

Summary Notes
The following will help you remember what to do at this step:

- What can you see on a natural level?
- What do you sense on a supernatural level? Ask God for scriptures, words of knowledge, insights, visions, images
- Just get the facts; not a medical interview or a counseling session
- Move to the next stage when you're ready.

STEP 2: THE DIAGNOSIS
"Why does this person have this condition?"

Now we can begin to identify the underlying issue we sense God is inviting us to pray for. We are asking, "Why does this person have this condition (or point of need)?"

There are many reasons someone might need prayer, and if the request is for physical healing, there may be a variety of reasons the person has a condition. The cause of a condition could be a) disease (natural causation – the person is just sick or has had an accident), b) sin (the person has committed a sin, or someone has sinned against them), c) emotional hurts (these can trigger physical symptoms), d) relationship problems (issues of unforgiveness or anger), or e) demonic influence (spiritual powers afflicting the person). Sometimes you may discern it is a combination of a few of these causes above. This is why we must depend on the Spirit – we don't want to be praying about one area for a person when the real issue is coming from something else.

Our goal is to see the person experience the depths of God's love, and to find freedom and healing in his or her heart, mind, and body. It is important to note here that in the Vineyard we see every person as a precious human being made in the image of God, who has chosen to be vulnerable in this moment of asking for prayer.

We never treat people as a project, or with indifference; we dignify people in the process of them seeking God for help. In ministry moments, the highest call of God on us is the second commandment – to love this person that He loves. Often people may not know the exact root of the problem. What they are asking for prayer about may not be the main issue God wants to address.

Ask the Holy Spirit to confirm if the person's analysis of the situation is accurate, or if there is something else He wants to reveal. People are complex, and the issues affecting their conditions can be just as complex.

A marriage may be in pain because of a childhood hurt. Bodies can be afflicted by psychosomatic illness, which is no less real in its impact than a disease. Holding resentment or bitterness toward another (living or dead) can cause distress that impacts a person emotionally and physically.

The interview concludes when we have determined what we believe to be the cause of the condition we are praying for.

Summary Notes

The following will help you remember what to do at this step:

- Are there natural causes here, such as a disease or accident?
- Is there sin involved, committed by the person or against the person?
- Are there emotional hurts causing physical symptoms?
- Are there relationship problems that are part of this issue?
- Is there demonic influence?
- Continue to ask God for help
- Ask more questions if it seems appropriate

STEP 3: PRAYER SELECTION
"What kind of prayer is needed to help this person?"

At this stage we are now asking, "What kind of prayer is needed to help this person?" and "Lord, (what) do you want to heal right now?"

We can assume that God wants to touch this person. However, He may not intend to heal the person in the way he or she desires. We want to agree with God in our prayers, rather than expecting God to agree with us on what *we* want to see happen. Having said this, we confidently pray for healing with 1 John 5:14-15 in mind – "This is the confidence we have in approaching God: that if we ask anything according to his will, he hears us. And if we know that he hears us — whatever we ask — we know that we have what we asked of him."

If we pray too generally, and with timidity, as if God probably doesn't want to do anything (or we don't want to look silly), then we probably won't see much happen. However, if we pray with confidence (without arrogance) and humility (without apology), led by the inner prompting of the Spirit, we are praying with the kind of confidence Jesus spoke of in Mark 11:24.

Wimber suggested that there are two categories into which healing prayers fall:

1. Prayers directed toward God
2. Words received from God

In the first, we are asking God how we should intercede for a sick person or a person requesting prayer. We are in a listening posture. Some choose to pray in tongues (1 Cor. 14:4) to make their hearts attentive and sensitive to God as they wait for insight from the Holy Spirit.

Prayers of intercession, in which we ask God to touch a person and the condition, may be the way the Spirit is inviting us to pray.

Sometimes God wants to speak something through us to the person. We may sense we are to pray prayers of command ("cancer, be gone in Jesus' name"), words of pronouncement ("I sense the Lord has healed you"), prayers of rebuke ("in Jesus' name, I rebuke the enemy" [Mark 9:25]), or prayers of agreement (agreeing with another person on your shared desire to see God's will accomplished [Matt. 18:19-20] in this person's life).

Ask God for wisdom, and believe you'll receive it. Leaning on the Holy Spirit, decide how you will pray, and move toward prayer engagement.

THE VINEYARD DNA

Summary Notes

The following will help you remember what to do at this step:

- Ask if the person is comfortable with the laying on of hands
- Ask the Holy Spirit to bring healing to the person
- Pray in the Spirit (pray in tongues as able)
- Consider the command of faith (Acts 3:6)
- Consider the pronouncement of faith (John 4:50)
- Consider the rebuke (breaking the power) of demonic influences; binding them (containing), or expelling them (getting rid of)

STEP 4: PRAYER ENGAGEMENT
"How effective are our prayers right now?"

This step consists of us moving into prayer, laying our hands on the person, and asking further interview questions as necessary.

Having decided how we will pray, we move forward, trusting we are sensing what the Father is doing in this person's life. As was noted in the previous step, we lay hands on the person if given permission. If there is a physical spot on the person's body that needs healing, we ask if we can lay hands on that part of the body (Luke 4:40). (When asking if we can lay hands on the person, we are always respectful. Helping him or her to feel safe aids the process.)

If the person is a member of the opposite sex, have someone of the person's own gender lay hands on them, or involve the spouse or friend. Wimber said, "It's important to treat people with respect so they may maintain their dignity" (*Power Healing*, p. 211).

In some cases, it may seem best to extend one's hands toward the person, rather than touching, especially if someone else is already laying hands on the person. As we begin, we may want to continually pray a prayer that has become vital in our Vineyard story: *"Come, Holy Spirit."*

This prayer is a simple invitation for the Spirit to do the work that only God can do. People may respond to the presence of the Spirit in various ways. They may remain quiet and still as we pray. They may experience warmth, or tingling in an area of the body, as prayer continues. As prayer is a power encounter between the overwhelming love of God and the enemy of our souls, there may be other manifestations such as trembling, shaking, weeping, laughing, or even falling over.

When people experience the peace and joy of God, breaking into their dire situation, there may be physical expressions that accompany the experience. Phenomena like these have occurred in revivals throughout church history, and may be one indicator that God's presence is being felt by the person. (Read *Power Healing*, p. 211-235, for more on manifestations during prayer.)

Continuing to listen to the Spirit as we pray, we ask God to pour more of His love into the person. We listen for revelation from God, and we follow those threads in our prayers. In the Vineyard, we often pray with our eyes open during personal ministry times. This is because we've become aware that some indications of effectiveness can be seen as we pray, while others cannot. When we sense we are finished praying, the person feels we are finished, or we have nothing left to pray, we let the person know we are finishing the prayer.

Summary Notes

The following will help you remember what to do at this step:

• Keep eyes open and watch for any effect (phenomenological signs like warmth, tingling, shaking)
• Ask questions of the person to find out what God might be doing
• Stop praying when a) the person thinks it's over, b) the Spirit tells you it's over, c) you've run out of things to pray, or d) it's going nowhere
• Remove your hands and talk to the person to indicate you are stopping

STEP 5: POST-PRAYER DIRECTION
"What should this person do to remain healed?" or **"What should this person do if he or she was not healed?"**

If the prayer focus is on physical healing, the results of healing prayer can be many. Offering some simple 'next step' direction may be helpful.

If the person was healed, or had a significant breakthrough in some area, encourage him or her to continue to walk closely with God, maintaining a rich life of worship, Bible reading, church connection, and avoidance of sin. You can also encourage the person to get the healing confirmed by a medical professional.

If a person was not healed, or did not have a significant breakthrough in their area of need, "...reassure them that God loves them and encourage them to seek more prayer" (*Power Healing*, p. 235).

For healing of the heart, mind, and body to be sustained, even after a moment of divine intervention, environments of committed Christian discipleship, accountability, and spiritual formation are necessary for ongoing growth.

If words or scriptures were received that were meaningful, encourage the person to write them down or record them so they can be referred to later.

God's intent in generously giving signs, wonders, miracles of healing, words of encouragement, words of knowledge, prophetic insights, and other gifts of love in times of prayer is that we would be drawn to love Him more, serving Him through a life of complete devotion.

Anything we can do to encourage someone to live out the greatest commandment, to "Love the Lord your God with all your heart and with all your soul and with all your mind and with all your strength" (Mark 12:30) is appropriate.

Summary Notes

The following will help you remember what to do at this step:

- Encourage the person to pursue continued prayer about the issue
- As necessary, call him or her to cease sinning (John 5:14; 8:11)
- Encourage the person to read the Scriptures and to nurture a deep relationship with God
- Encourage them to stay active in a local church community
- Visit their doctor, if a healing occurred, to confirm the healing

THE FIVE STEP PRAYER MODEL: A REVIEW

01 THE INTERVIEW
Introduce yourself, then ask, "How can I pray for you?" or "Where does it hurt?" This is not a medical interview, but rather an opportunity to listen as we assess the person's need.

02 THE DIAGNOSIS
"Why does this person have this condition?" Identify the underlying issue you sense God is inviting you to pray for. It could be physical, emotional, relational, or otherwise.

03 PRAYER SELECTION
"What kind of prayer is needed to help this person?" You can also ask, "Lord, (what) do you want to heal right now?" Consider prayers of intercession, command, pronouncement, rebuke (of demonic influences), and agreement.

04 PRAYER ENGAGEMENT
"How effective are our prayers right now?" Move into prayer, laying hands on the person (respectfully and by invitation), and asking further interview questions as necessary. Pray according to your diagnostic decision and prayer selection, listening to the Spirit.

05 POST-PRAYER DIRECTION
"What should this person do to remain healed?" or "What should this person do if he or she was not healed?" Offer some simple direction to the person who was prayed for. Encourage him or her to receive more prayer.

Encourage the person to nurture a deep relationship with God, to stay in the Scriptures, to remain in fellowship, and to turn away from sin. If a healing occurred, encourage him or her to get confirmation from a medical professional. Finally, encourage them to document what God did. Trust God to use you in prayer – and expect the Kingdom to come!

WANT TO KNOW MORE ABOUT THE VINEYARD?

The following books, along with many others, offer helpful perspectives on the history and practices of the Vineyard Movement.

The Quest For The Radical Middle
Bill Jackson

Power Healing
John Wimber

Power Evangelism
John Wimber

Wimber's audio teaching and many other books on the Vineyard Movement can be purchased by contacting:

Vineyard Resources
W www.vineyardresources.com
P 1-800-852-8463

For digital resources for all the ministries in your church, from the Kingdom heart of the Vineyard, join:

Vineyard Digital Membership
www.vineyarddigitalmembership.com